LAND ROVER LRO Magazine Restoration TIPS & TECHNIQUES

COMPILED BY RICHARD GREEN

ISBN 1 85520 181X

Published by

LRO PUBLICATIONS LTD.

Distributed by

Brooklands Books Ltd., PO Box 146, Cobham, Surrey KT11 1LG, England.

Printed in Hong Kong

INTRODUCTION

As anyone who owns an elderly Land-Rover knows, taking it apart and putting it back together again are not just things you do to keep it on the road; they are part of the fun of ownership. They aren't always as much fun as they could be, though. When the workshop manual tells you that reassembly is the reverse of dismantling, it doesn't tell you all the things that an experienced Land-Rover mechanic would if he were watching over your shoulder. Finding out the hard way that reassembly is just a tiny bit more complicated than the manual suggests can be one of the less enjoyable aspects of playing with a Land-Rover.

For that reason, a lot of people were only too pleased to read David Bowyer's series of articles on rebuilding a Series III model in Land Rover Owner. These articles told the plain truth about the problems of dismantling and reassembly, in the words of someone who had done the job. The only problem was, if you were following the sequence through from start to finish, you had to wait a month between each of the episodes. Now that Brooklands Books have republished the whole series in a single volume, a whole lot more people are going to be able to benefit from it . . . . and they won't have to wait fourteen months to read the final episode, either!

That isn't all, though. In this book, LRO's Richard Green has pulled together a fine collection of other how-to articles from the magazine. You want to fit a winch? You want to drop in a V8 engine? Try reading articles written by those who've actually done it. It's almost as good as having that experienced Land-Rover mechanic looking over your shoulder.

James Taylor

DISTRIBUTED BY

Brooklands Books Ltd., PO Box 146, Cobham, Surrey KT11 1LG, England
Telephone: 0932 865051 Fax: 0932 868803

Brooklands Books Ltd., 1/81 Darley St., PO Box 199, Mona Vale, NSW 2103, Australia
Telephone: 2 997 8428 Fax: 2 452 4679

Motorbooks International, Osceola, Wisconsin 54020, U.S.A.
Telephone: 715 294 3345 Fax: 715 294 4448

Printed in Hong Kong

CONTENTS

Part One

Series III Refurbishing Project

Part Two

Land Rover Tips and Techniques

Photographs on pages 4-58 have been taken by David Bowyer and those on pages 60-64 by Chris Bennett.
We are indebted to both of them for our front and back cover pictures.

First in a new series by David Bowyer

△ *As delivered: apart from the front offside wing the panels are encouragingly straight. Purchased from Winston Pincombe Land Rovers for about £1,000, KYJ has some 94,000 miles on the clock.*

Refurbishing a Series III

THINKING of buying a 'middle of the road' Land Rover? Perhaps you are new to Land Rovers and itching to get your hands on something to 'do up'.

Perhaps you have been into Land Rovers and Range Rovers for many years and are looking for a challenge and 'er in doors likes the idea of having her own.

Perhaps a son or daughter has shared your enthusiassm over the years as they have been growing up, are about to take their Driving Test and are looking for their own transport. Mum and Dad like the idea of them owning something 'rather sturdy', easy to maintain and repair with parts readily available, and a vehicle quite happy to stand outside all year.

A good starter, a people and load carrier, will tow just about anything asked of it and relatively cheap to insure.

Whatever your reason, your desires, your thoughts on body types and styles, you have several considerations. The first is, of course, your budget starting with your initial capital outlay, making due allowance for refurbishing the Land Rover to make it a safe and reliable vehicle for all the family to use.

You may also have to allow for many mechanical and chassis repairs depending on the age of the vehicle, and the type of usage it has had during its life. Perhaps the vehicle's regular servicing has left a lot to be desired. Wouldn't it be nice to have it resprayed, and take it on holiday, put the luggage and mountain bikes on the roof rack. The thoughts are endless.

With these ideas in mind, LRO decided to set a budget figure of £2,500 for the purchase and repair/refurbishment for a typical Land Rover that would appeal to many of its readers. That's where I come in. Living and working in deepest Devon, I'm given the task of finding a suitable 'middle of the road' vehicle.

There are, of course, many readers who would be happy doubling the budget and simply go out and buy a ready refurbished vehicle from one of the many highly respected advertisers in LRO. An 'off the shelf' or 'rebuilt to a specification' vehicle

△ *A fifteen year old vehicle, she is basically solid, but closer inspection reveals rust in the rear cross member.*

is ideal for those who have too little time, or insufficient knowledge, to carry out most of the necessary work. Buying this way also gives peace of mind as Land Rover specialists give either 3, 6 or even 12 months parts warranty and possibly labour as well depending on the amount of refurbishment on the vehicle in question.

Some specialists go the whole hog and do a complete rebuild from the chassis upwards, often starting with a brand new galvanised chassis and replacing every single component that shows the slightest sign of wear. You therefore get a virtually 'new' vehicle, but your bill might be three to four times our project vehicle budget.

Having established the bodystyle to look for, how do you find one? Well, of course the first place to look is in LRO. Lots and lots of ads, Dealer ads, small ads, ads with photos. Lots of smiles. 'One owner', 'never been used off road', 'carefully maintained', 'used for shopping only'.

Scour the other mags too for possibilities, likewise 'Exchange and Mart', 'Autotrader' and similar publications. Even your local or county newspaper and free advertising type papers can give you ideas.

It's 'ideas' you are looking for, or rather comparisons between styles, ages and conditions, based on your budget. Make up a schedule. Take a piece of A4 ruled paper, or several come to that, and list your requirements, and alternatives. As Land Rovers are really giant Meccano sets you can swap 'soft tops', 'hard tops', 'hardtops with windows', 'safari tops', 'tropical tops', 'alpine lights', 'tailgates', 'safari rear doors', 'seats', 'spare wheel mounting positions' and so on. You may be liable however to the authorities for a proportion of VAT and car tax if you install side windows in a hard top.

As I was given a free hand by LRO as to what type of Land Rover to buy, I considered that a SWB late Series IIA or an early Series III would be ideal. Many will say that the IIA was the last traditional Land Rover built with its centre binical encompassing the instrument gauges, parcel shelf to either side and above, good

▷

◁ *These seats will need more than a re-trim! A set of County seats would look much better.*

It will make more sense to replace the damaged panels than to ▽ *attempt a repair.*

old fashioned single speed windscreen wipers, Smiths 'round' heater, and a wire spoked steering wheel.

Others would prefer a Series III with its more 'modern' interior, instrument gauges in front of the driver and associated switches and controls, a more useful parcel shelf and padded protection above, twin speed wipers and a much better heating and demister system. Over the many years of Land Rovering, having owned both Series IIA and III vehicles, I like both. Come to that I'm rather partial to Series Ones and Nineties too!

I spent much time in browsing through the various publications listing on my schedule the years down one side starting with 1968 and finishing with 1976 to give me an eight year period to choose from. Along the top of my sheets of paper a series of prices starting with £800 and rising to £1,600 in £100 increments.

Then taking the information gleaned from adverts I'm able to list possibilities down across the pages on what's on offer by way of age, various asking prices, along with notes on body styles, condition and special features. I ended up of course with reams of paper, but that's the fun of it, and you learn lots too. This really is an ideal way of getting a feeling of what you can get at what price.

On the subject of asking price there is nearly always an opportunity to haggle. I did! By now you can choose some vehicles from your shortlist to telephone about with a view of going to inspect.

A few things to consider. The cost of travelling great distances often to no avail; don't buy without a thorough inspection after having a good road test, and finally buying from a reputable dealer can give you a warranty — unless you have bought at rock bottom price!

Remember, there are plenty of fishes in the sea, so don't buy the first vehicle you see, unless you are really sure.

Decision time

As you can see from the photographs accompanying this article we decided to plumb for this quite nice Series III which was manufactured early in 1976. That makes her 15 years old, but that's nothing

△ It's all there but a thorough clean may reveal more.

Both driver and passenger doors will need to be re-trimmed. ▷

After the underside has been carefully cleaned, a closer ▽ inspection can be carried out.

for a Land Rover.

The vehicle was purchased in fact from one of our regular advertisers in LRO, Winston Pincombe, The Garage, Chulmeigh just 20 miles away from my base in Devon. After a suitable realistic price was agreed, it was arranged to have the vehicle delivered just a couple of days before the heavy snow hit us in early February.

A close inspection of KYJ 57P revealed that much attention was needed to the chassis, mechanics and interior trim. It was a typical example of a vehicle that's done its various owners proud over fifteen years. What appealed to me was that 'she' was a 'complete' vehicle with a 'sweet running' engine. A Hard Top with a Tropical Roof and a Safari rear door makes her an ideal candidate for fitting side windows in the future together with rear seats.

The offside front wing needs replacing, just like the current Land Rover Parts advert. There are holes galore in the chassis which require plating, various bushes are worn, the shock absorbers are 'shot', one of the gearbox mountings is broken, much wear in propshafts and U/Js. An overdrive is fitted, but the gearstick for it is lying in the parcelshelf. All three front seats need replacing, likewise the door trims and floor covering, together with a whole list of smaller items.

In the months to come I will lead you through the necessary repair works using both our facilities and those of a Land Rover Specialist to carry out the major items where I don't have either the skill or special tools to tackle the work. Naturally, I will lead you through a complete service which should automatically cover every type of checking and adjustment and changing fluids.

Finally, after changing that damaged wing and fitting the side windows, we will rub down, prepare as necessary and spray the outside of the vehicle to give that 'finishing touch'. And with a new set of tyres she will be ready to give sterling service.

My next article in this series will tell you what to look out for when buying a series II, IIA or III. Now where did I put that wire brush? . . . .

Buyer beware

HAVING NOW fuelled you and the family with thoughts on buying a suitable 'middle of the road' Land Rover. Let's take a closer look at what problems and faults you are likely to find when looking at possible buys.

I am going to assume that most people contemplating buying a 15-20 year old Land Rover will opt for a two and a quarter litre petrol model. These are more readily available and easier and cheaper to work on and maintain than the diesel. The family will find the vehicle more pleasant to drive, too.

From your shortlist you start making arrangements to go and visit various vehicles within a sensible distance. You are told on the phone beforehand by the seller: "lovely vehicle, drives well, had loads of money spent on 'her' during last year . . . and many new spares have been fitted too." Ask the seller exactly what work has been done, what new spares were fitted, when and by whom.

This is important in fathoming out the vehicle's history, especially when the general concensus of opinion in the family is "if we are getting a Land Rover and doing it up, we should be able to keep it for years and years!"

With this in mind it is up to you to make sure you get a good'n. If you are told over the phone that various work has been done and a whole load of new spares fitted, then make notes so that when inspecting the vehicle you can check out the truth.

Be prepared when making visits to view Land Rovers. For a start arrange your visit during daylight hours. Trying to poke around a vehicle in darkness with just the aid of a torch isn't going to help a lot.

Take a large old mat 6 or 7 feet long by 3 feet wide to lay on when sprawling around under the said vehicle. A screw-driver and hammer to poke around under the chassis is useful. Please ask permission before digging in, especially if the seller is standing by your feet! Personally, I prefer the owner to go and make a cup of tea when I start investigating a chassis.

If your are really going to be meticulous about it, a wire brush isn't going to go amiss either, but do wear some goggles for obvious reasons. Remember too, you don't know the vehicle at this stage so if the ground's not dead level then for safety's sake, if the hand brake isn't too good, check the wheels before going underneath.

Even though it's daylight still carry a torch as it helps to carry out a proper investigation in poor light.

If you have a friend who is a knowledgeable sort of chap, especially on Land Rovers, then ask him along too. It could be the cheapest pint you've bought him yet.

Finally, don't forget to take your notes, overalls, a rag or two both for wiping hands and checking fluids — and perhaps the camera too.

Make sure, too, that you know exactly where the vehicle is. Now, don't laugh but quite often people selling their Land Rover privately just happen to live down "the narrow lane just past the third farmhouse after leaving the village towards . . . ." The number of times I've spent hours to find the owner's house is nobody's business. So, take a tip from me, get a map to the phone when you are being told where to meet. You'll need all the time you can get when you are there, so don't waste it.

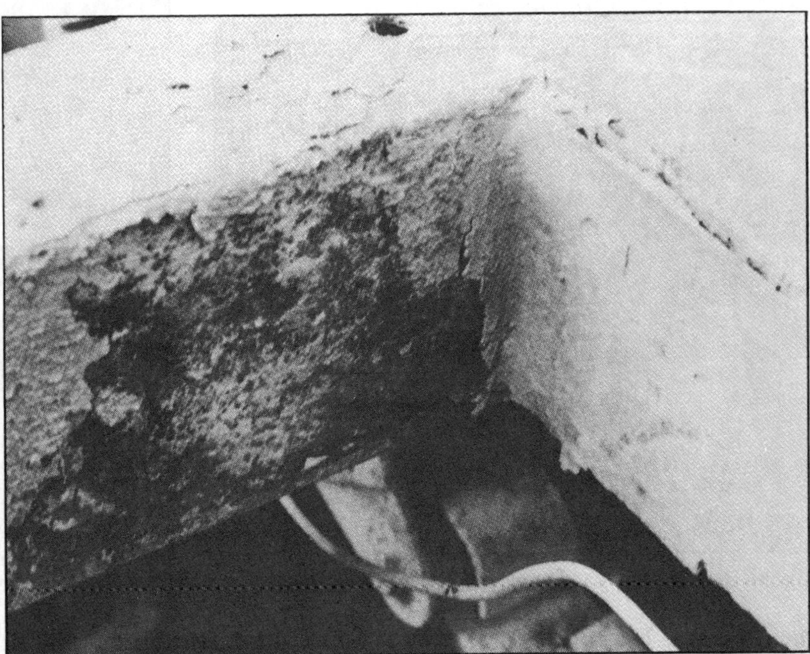

△ The pictures on these and following pages are not of our Series III project vehicle but serve to show some of the nasties that can await you when you're looking for a Land Rover of more mature years. Above can be seen a rusting gap between the plated repairs and original steel of this centre crossmember.

The inspection

On arrival you'll have your first chance to see the vehicle and give her the once over. Round the side, quick, look over the bonnet, round the front, looks good. Back to the driver's door, unlock it and jump into the seat to look around inside.

You put the key into the ignition, pull out the choke and start the engine. The engine splutters into life quite quickly, into gear, let the clutch out cautiously and you slowly move the vehicle a few feet.

You ponder for a while with the gear stick in neutral. The handbrake lever seems to come a long way up, you listen to the purring engine, bit of a rattle arising from the gearbox.

You glance around the inside. It looks all there, bit tatty, odd wires hanging down. It's quite nice you think. Well it's a Land Rover isn't it, full of character.

You're still thinking and dreaming "is this it — the one for me", then there's a tap on the window. "Tea's ready, got her started O.K. then, she's always started well."

You shut off the engine, climb out and take a good look at the outside from all round. Supping your tea you politely ask

△ *This chassis must have been 'past it' many years ago*

The chassis here is well rusted under the spring hangers ▷

a few questions relating to the various work carried out on the vehicle. The answers given seem fairly honest.

Now I've been down this road many, many times over an equal number of years and I don't care what anyone says. It's first impressions that count. Within the very first few minutes, even seconds, you may like the vehicle, you may like it a lot. You may just screw up your eyes a little and try to imagine what the vehicle might look like after months of sweat and tears. You could be thinking: "no I'll go and see the next one."

My suggestion is, whatever your thoughts, don't make up your mind until you've had a good poke around. The owner no doubt will be most pleased to give his permission to carry out a full inspection, he may even help by offering to get you another cup of tea! This is your chance to rapidly put your overalls on, slide the bit of carpet under, tools in hand, and goggles too.

Now, you are starting with the chassis in the inspection because, quite frankly, the chassis is a rather important part of the vehicle. Don't worry if you find some rust, that is to be expected. Small holes can be repaired, but if there are signs of the chassis totally collapsing then that's a major problem.

Start by checking the rear cross member. Is it square to the back of the vehicle? You are looking for signs of damage caused by lots of heavy towing. A deep drop plate, with tow ball mounted low, can cause horrible strain damage on the cross member.

Check for rust in the member itself especially along the bottom. Tap with the hammer, poke with the screwdriver, wire brush it a little if you like. Check the various drainage holes to see if they are still round or have they rusted out to larger uneven holes? Has the cross member been plated?

Working forward, check the welds between the cross member and main chassis rails, then onto the spring hangers. Any signs of holes here will definitely cause an MOT failure. Poke around underneath the chassis and up around the sides; again check for signs of plating.

Check the forward spring hangers of the rear springs then work along the chassis towards the gearbox. Consider for a while that most rust problems are caused through water being trapped 'inside' the chassis. Therefore, the steel normally rusts from the inside out.

Keep tapping and poking away, checking the middle crossmembers and outriggers on the way. You are not only looking for rust in the chassis and adjoining components, but also for any problems with chassis joints falling apart through faulty welding repairs or fatigue.

By this stage you will probably get out from under the vehicle and shake the dust, mud or oil out of your hair. You query with the owner about some of the repairs carried out. He probably doesn't know too much about it; a friend of a friend got it through the MOT.

You get back under and check the bulkhead outriggers and your eyes glance up at the footwells — oh dear. We'll come back to that later.

Check the spring hangers supporting both the rear and front of the front axle springs, working finally to the front dumb irons on to which the bumper mounts.

Only you can tell how good — or bad the chassis is. If it is really rotten through and through then it may be best to give the vehicle a miss. Plenty more to go and see.

After stretching the neck, we dive back under again, this time starting at the front to check visually the general state of the underside. First the front springs, do they look good or otherwise? Perhaps heavy rust is blowing the leaves of the springs apart. If so replacement is the only answer.

Whilst here, what's the condition of the front axle, is the diff casing in good order and not dented. Are there signs of any oil seeping from the diff pinion. Also check the surrounding swivel housings, are the swivels clean and polished or are they badly pitted and horrible?

Take a look at the steering relay, does it look rusted or has the bottom oil seal gone? Look too at the track rod ends and condition of the brake pipes and shock absorbers. Are the bump stops still in place?

Moving back, give the front propshaft a good nudge. Does it feel loose? What are the UJs like? Check too the exhaust ▷

system, general condition of the engine sump, bell housing, gearbox, transfer case and handbrake.

Whilst in this area look closely at the fuel tank for signs of damage. Check the rear propshaft and UJs for slackness and on the rear axle look for signs of pinion seal seepage and general condition of the axle and diff casing, along with brake pipes, rear springs, bump stops, and shock absorbers.

Check the exhaust right through to the back. Also cast your eyes back along the chassis to inspect the brake pipes for corrosion and security of fitment against the chassis.

After checking that little lot you should have a general idea of the condition and previous usage of the vehicle. If the underside is clean, reasonably rust-free and tidy with all items in place and very little oil seepage from the axles, engine and transmission, then one could hope the vehicle has been well cared for.

If your investigation shows that the whole of the underside is rusty, caked in mud and oil, everything loose, blown springs and what have you, then maybe you should look for something better to buy.

△ *A typically rusted rear cross member. See that rust in the PTO hole . . .*

▽ *. . . and the end is well beyond repair.*

Under the bonnet

Assuming that it's not too bad, it's time to get one's head under the bonnet. Take a long look into the engine compartment. Does it look complete? You can always tell if things aren't quite right, trailing wires, missing pipes, bits cobbled together, holes in the bulkhead, battery clamp missing.

Is the engine generally clean and oil-free? Or is it caked in oil and grease? Again a clean engine speaks volumes for its previous care.

Check the oil for level and colour. You can tell whether it's been changed recently or not. Check too the radiator level and it's colour. Of course, it has antifreeze/inhibitor in it hasn't it?

Look closely into and through the radiator core. Any signs of weeping? Look for signs of water seepage from the various gaskets around the engine.

Start the engine and have a good listen. Have a feel for where the rattles and knocks, if any, are coming from.

Memorise the odd noises because later on after a thorough road test when the engine's fully warmed up you'll be having a good listen again. What was the colour of the exhaust when you fired up the engine? Did it look normal, black or water dripping out the end? Again if the engine sounds and looks knackered, you could not be blamed for looking for something else to buy.

If, like the underside, you are pleasantly surprised then you could be on to a winner. The next item to check is the bulkhead between the vehicle's interior and engine compartment. This could be a shock!

Lift out any carpeting or matting, carefully move back any bulkhead trim if fitted like on the station wagons and have a close inspection of the footwells. Too often the rust bug gets into these sections.

They are, of course, repairable if attacked by rust, but what is more of a problem to repair is the outside edges of the bulkhead being the door pillars.

Have a careful tap round with the screwdriver. Have a good check around the top of the bulkhead too, under the windscreen and the surrounding areas to the front hinged vents. Rust in this area is again a problem to repair easily.

If you are reasonably satisfied in this bulkhead area then we are getting on well.

It is now time to have a good look at the general interior of the vehicle. Most parts like the seats, trim, fixtures and fittings are very easy to obtain and replace. Do the doors open and close easily?

If a truck cab, hard top or station wagon are all the keys there, including the duplicate set and do they all work? Check too the door tops as they are prone to rust, but are easy to replace.

Does the outside of the Land Rover need much working on? Are all the panels generally straight including the roof? Small dents are easy to repair, but large gouges and buckles require replacement panels.

Check the tyres for sidewall cuts and general tread damage including the spare. Slowly turn the steering wheel from side to side, feeling for any excessive play. A little play is acceptable. Grab each road wheel in turn and give a good shake to give an impression of possible wheel bearing wear, or front swivel pin wear.

Well, if you are still interested in the Land Rover and the owner hasn't thrown a wobbly watching you meticulously check over his vehicle, then now's the time to ask if you could kindly have a drive.

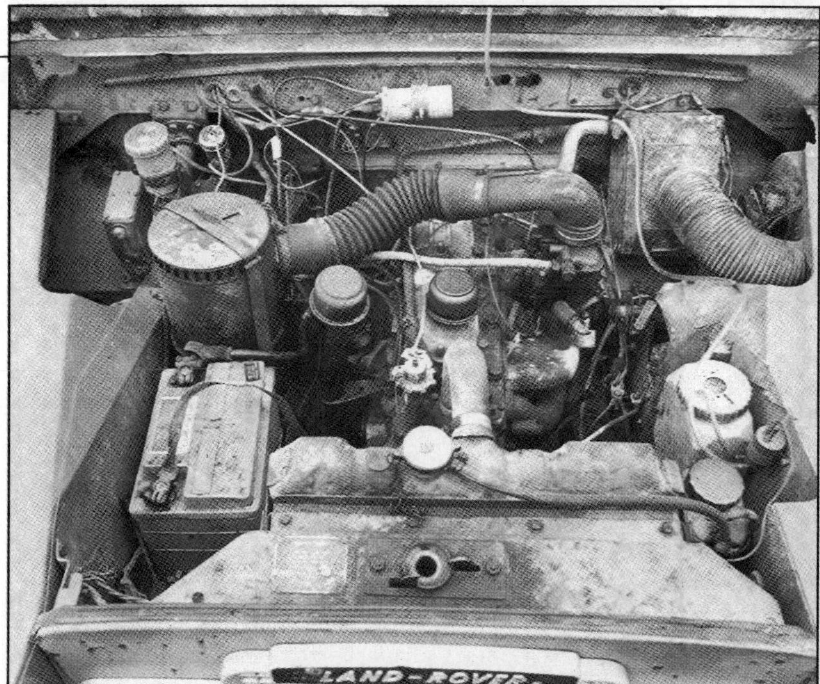

△ *A well-cobbled engine bay of a Series III. It has all the appearance of being abused and 'worked on'.*

Typical bulkhead problems in the footwell and door pillar areas. It's been plated before and the door pillar is collapsing. ▷

Before driving off you must consider the legal angle of the insurance cover. Quite simply are you covered to drive the vehicle? If not you'll have to rely on the owner giving you an on-road demonstration leaving you to drive around his yard. Also is the vehicle fully taxed and does it have a current MOT. You only have to ask to see the MOT certificate and a glance at the window will reveal all. If it is a dealer you are visiting, no doubt he will be using trade plates.

It also wouldn't be a bad idea to check the operation of the handbrake, footbrake, clutch, windscreen wipers, mirrors and lights, especially the brake lights. If you get stopped for any reason, ignorance will be no excuse.

Whilst driving along keep you ears well pinned back for any unusual noises. Generally Land Rovers, especially 15-20 year old examples make plenty of noise. But it's the 'whines' and 'clunks' you are listening for.

Train your ears down to the rear diff through the back floor, the gear box and transfer case down beside you. The engine may have run sweet in the yard, but what's it like at the upper end of the speed range?

Does she pull nicely in all gears from rest, with no notching or cranking? If overdrive is fitted does that operate smoothly as well, or does it whine like hell hanging on the back of the transmission. Remember that the overdrive should only be used in third and top gear in high ratio. Do the brakes work well and pull you up evenly?

Find a quiet bit of a straight country lane and in each gear gently rock the vehicle backwards and forwards on the throttle as you drive along to simulate pulling and alternative overrunning in order to listen to funny noises and possible jumping out of gear in an overrun mode. But please not only warn the owner, but ask him if you may do this. If not, you may give him a shocking experience.

Now it's time to check the operation of the four wheel drive. To do this there is no need to attempt any aggressive off roading. Simply find a track in the area where you have a right to drive. I'm sure the owner will know of a legal place to drive especially if he's a farmer. All you want to establish is that everything works O.K.

First engage the front free wheel hubs if fitted and make sure the overdrive, again if fitted, is out of gear. To operate 4 wheel drive in high ratio simply push down the yellow knob, preferably while stationary, and move off along the track.

You will feel a definite tautness in the steering showing that the front axle is doing it's job. Keep an ear open for any peculiar noises as the front axle is brought into play through being driven from the gearbox.

Having satisfied yourself that all is well in high ratio, now *stop* to engage low ratio. Pull the red lever back through neutral, into the low ratio position, pulling back this lever automatically pops the yellow lever back up.

Be warned, let the clutch out slowly, if you haven't driven a Land Rover before in low ratio, as you can lurch forward.

As you move off through the gears along the track or across the fields, no doubt your enthusiasm may get the better of you. *Don't over do it.* The owner probably won't let you anyway.

Simply prove to yourself that the four wheel drive high and low ratios work. Be sure to push the red lever back through neutral to the upright position as you arrive back onto a hard surface. Any attempt to use four wheel drive on a hard surface can break transmission components through 'wind up' between the front and rear axles as you turn corners.

Haggling

Well, if you are satisfied with this test together with the general condition of the whole vehicle and there are no dramatic 'whines' or 'clunks' and 'she' steers reasonably well then it's probably back to the owner's home to 'discuss' that asking price. It's all down to you to pay what you think is a sensible price for the vehicle.

After all, you've made several comparisons between plenty of vehicles that have been advertised. But you have also probably realised by now that you get what you pay for. One thing's certain, you don't pay pro-rata on age.

You are paying on condition and the variance is enormous. You either 'buy for a song' and pay for it later through specialist labour, spares and frustration or pay well for a good example which needs little time or spares spent on it.

It's your choice. You must bear in mind

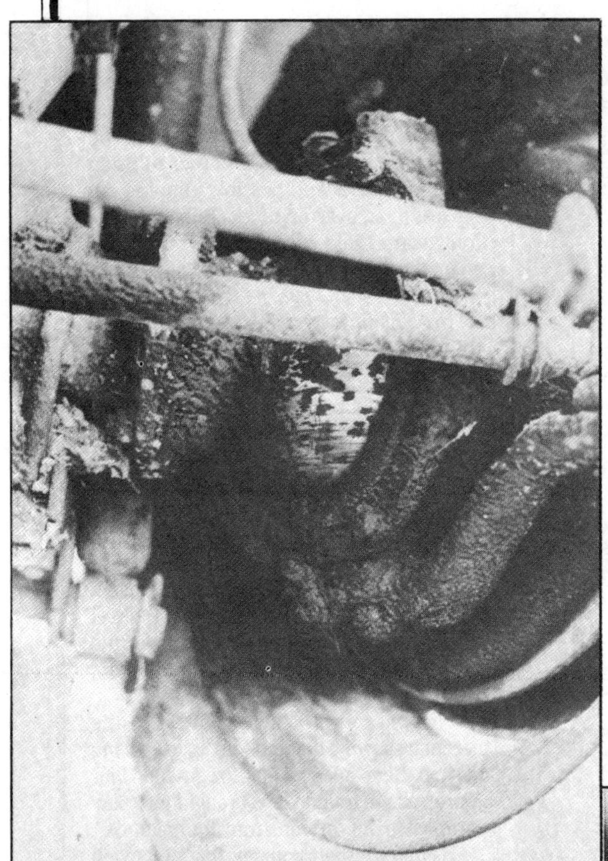

△ *Viewed from outside, this bulkhead door pillar is finished.*

◁ *Front swivel housings like this will have to be replaced.*

△ *These springs are 'shot'. Rust has formed between each leaf making them blow apart.*

your capabilities as a home mechanic or your resources to pay for work to be done. If you are going to attempt to do most of the work yourself, other than specialist repairs, then allow a goodly sum over the top of buying the vehicle to carry out such work.

If you are still uncertain about this particular vehicle, but think it's the one for you, you could always get a second opinion from one or two friends. On the other hand, if you are not too happy with her don't worry, there are plenty more fish in the sea, so to speak.

The story I've told you is typical of buying from a private individual. The same can apply when buying from a dealer. Still check out as much as you can. You may of course be paying more, but, on the other hand, you get some sort of minimal guarantee. I know of one jovial dealer who is known to say "Well my lad, if you want a guarantee, then it's once round the field or half way round if it's a big field".

From whomever you decide to purchase, don't part with any money until all the documents are to hand. You have been warned.

Finally, after closing the deal and before driving the vehicle home, don't forget to get the appropriate insurance cover and have a friend follow you back. Give your newly purchased vehicle the once over again including checking the tyre pressures and the tightness of the wheel nuts. I'll relate a story to you about wheel nuts one day.

In next month's article we will totally clean our vehicle 'KYJ 57P" and report on a thorough investigation in the workshop on a full list of what we expect to need to do to the vehicle in order to give her a new lease of life.

Happy hunting.

My grateful thanks to James Radley of the Lincolnshire Land Rover Club for providing some of the accompanying photographs and to Winston Pincombe for allowing me to photograph some of his vehicles in his Land Rover 'graveyard'.

Prepare to start

Power washing and degreasing are essential before work can begin.

I WILL assume that you have now finally made your choice and have taken delivery of the vehicle. If you have paid heed to what I've told you, then you will have made the right decision.

Perhaps I am still whetting your appetite, and if that is so, it could be to your advantage, to hang on for a little longer. What's the hurry when you have so much choice available to you. And, by following this series, I sincerely hope you have a better insight into what lies ahead.

So, where do we start? Well, I suggest that if you are fairly new to Land Rovers and therefore possibly uncertain what belongs where and where to look at what, then buy some manuals covering the vehicle. And where is the best place to order manuals from then? The LRO Bookshop of course! Your contact is Anne Cornwall and you will find the available list of books at the back of each LRO.

Our project vehicle is a Series III, so, naturally one needs specific manuals to cover the vehicle in question. There are three books you really ought to own if you are contemplating carrying out any of the work yourself.

Without question the small A5 sized 'Owners Manual' is the one to start with, as it will help to familiarise you with the vehicle. The information given covers both petrol and diesel models and is divided into several sections to facilitate reference to any particular aspect of the Land Rover.

Sections One to Four cover driving the vehicle, gear changing procedure, the use of instruments and various controls, heating system, running requirements and a service guide. These sections should be carefully studied so that you not only get the best out of the vehicle in terms of economical and efficient operation, but also to obtain maximum pleasure and enjoyment when driving both on and off road.

Subsequent sections include detailed instructions for the necessary maintenance and adjustments which should be carried out at regular intervals, together with fault finding and specifications of the vehicle. All in all, a very useful book to carry in the

Land Rover, especially if you are 'new to the game'. At over 160 pages and costing just £10 you will find it a most useful reference guide.

If you are contemplating carrying out more than just general maintenance and you feel that you have sufficient skills to be more adventurous, then it will pay you to order the excellent 'Repair Operation Manual', again published by Land Rover Ltd. This very thorough book covers every conceivable part of the vehicle in great depth, starting with general data, engine tuning, torque wrench settings, general fitting instructions (very important for your safety) and further covers maintenance schedules and recommended lubricants in greater depth.

The remainder of the manual covers all you will ever really need to know about your vehicle, how to dismantle, replace and reassemble, along with numerous illustrations to help you identify the work being carried out. The book is nearly an inch thick and at around £20 it could save you a fortune in giving you the knowledge in how to go about the work yourself.

Now, if you really want a complete reference library on your 'new' vehicle, then you will find the official 'Parts Catalogue' very useful. The book, about one and a half inches in thickness is entirely made up of exploded view illustrations of just about every part of the vehicle along with part numbers attached to each item. Without doubt, the owning of this book, greatly simplifies the identifying, and therefore ordering, of any originally fitted items or parts of the Land Rover, right down to the last nut, bolt and washer.

What I like out of the Parts Catalogues is the very clear illustrations showing you exactly in what order the individual components within the various assemblies go together. This is definitely a bonus, believe me. Also for those interested, many of the optional accessories are included as well. A trifle more expensive at around £27, but think of the knowledge you could gain.

The LRO Bookshop also stock what is known as service training literature. These are specialised publications for those who are completely stripping down and rebuilding engines, gearboxes and axles.

The Bookshop also stocks a similar full range of reference books for Series I, II, IIA, 101, 90, 110, Range Rover and Discovery, along wth many useful general books on the subject.

Before moving on and whilst still on the subject of manuals, general fitting instructions and procedure, I would like to take this opportunity of giving you a firm WARNING. Now, I know all LRO readers are sensible people, but as they say "listen carefully, because I shall say this only once!"

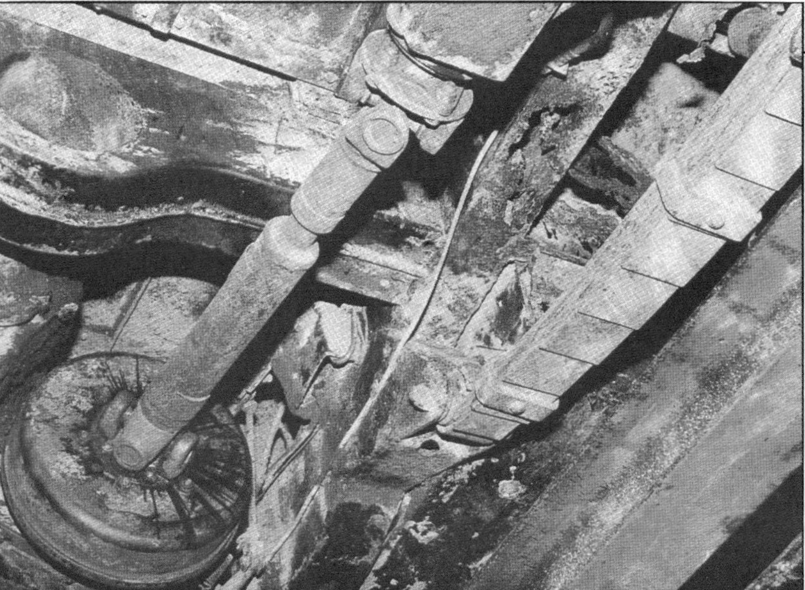

△ *A common problem: main chassis rails rust from the inside out.*
▽ *Spring bushes are checked for wear by using a pry bar.*

If you are going to carry out any work on either the steering, suspension or braking system of a Land Rover (or any other vehicle come to that) yourself, you have an obligation to carry out such work with the most meticulous care. Always be certain that you have done the work in accordance with the workshop manual right down to the last word. Know what you are doing, and check again after you have done the job. None of the work is difficult and is well within the scope of most enthusiasts.

In the case of steering, always use genuine parts, especially replacement track rod ends and be conscious of possible damage caused by excessive off roading. Suspension bushes must be in first class order and there must be absolutely no sign of looseness with regard to the 'U' bolts attaching the axles to the leaf springs.

As regards the braking system — both the footbrakes and handbrake — it is imperative that both are operating absolutely correctly. The vehicle must pull up evenly, and progressively, with no hint of any juddering. The handbrake must hold the vehicle securely, even on a steep hill.

All those three areas of importance can easily be worked on by the average Land Rover enthusiast. But take your time and follow the written procedures.

I will always remember this story from a few years ago. I was waiting outside the classroom for my visitors to arrive for the first day of one of our courses. Across the valley I could hear a general commotion in the vicinity of the steep windy hill leading down to us. Then a vehicle came flying up our drive with the driver re-

△ *All the outriggers, like the main chassis, are checked for soundness. James highlights the rusted rear crossmember by putting a welding hammer* ▽ *through it!*

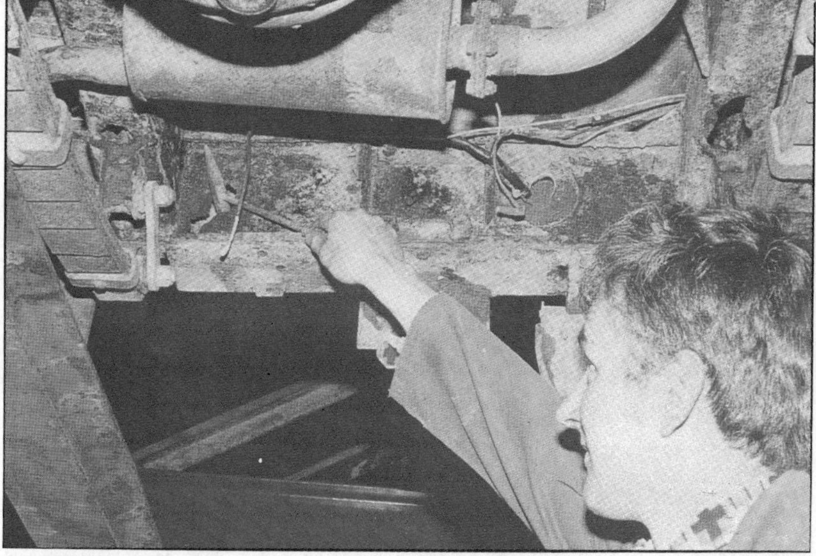

questing urgent help for the vehicle following him down the hill which had crashed on the bend.

Keith, my co-instructor accompanied me to the incident only to find out that an expedition prepared 109 Series III complete with roof rack, jerry cans, and roof tent was lying upside down held up by the banks across the lane. Fortunately all the occupants had climbed out without a scratch or a bruise. But the poor Land Rover was wrecked.

With the use of two winches and a high lift jack, we got the vehicle back onto it's wheels facing down the hill and towed it down to our workshop.

It didn't take very long to establish the cause of the accident. The brake fluid reservoir, bolted to a bracket attached to the plate mounted on the top of the clutch pedal box, had come adrift. This allowed the reservoir to fall over sideways coming down the first part of the hill loosing brake fluid. The six screws holding down the plate were missing giving the impression that some repair works had just been carried out. On asking, yes, repairs had been carried out the day before. A clutch master cylinder had been changed under that plate securing the reservoir.

I phoned the garage who carried out the work the day before. He sent a transporter down immediately to collect the vehicle and I understand he spent the following week completely rebuilding the Land Rover prior to the group leaving for Africa. All that risk and cost to him, because a second check wasn't made after working on part of the brake system. I bet he never forgets to replace those six small screws!

Preparation

Enough said, let's start preparing our project vehicle. I don't know about you, but I like to be able to see 'all' the underside of a Land Rover when I'm making a list of what needs doing and what spares are wanted. Over all the years that I've been involved with buying old Land Rovers, my first job is cleaning the underside thoroughly.

Not everyone is going to have their own power washing facilities. You could always solder a plumbers copper plate blanking cap onto a piece of ½″ (13mm) copper pipe secured into the end of the garden hose with jubilee clips. In the end of the cap drill a very small hole to allow the water to escape as a powerful jet. The hole being enlarged slightly if the jet is too small. The beauty of this home made lance is you can reach well under and all round especially if you bend the end of the copper pipe a little. Or simply use a garden hose jet.

Cold water pressure cleaners like ours can be hired at a very reasonable cost from your local hire centre. Full blown steam cleaners may be hired too, but are much more expensive.

I prefer the cold water cleaners using a well tried and tested method of vehicle cleaning which you can use whether you have made your own lance or have the use of a pressure cleaner like ours. Pop along to your local automotive parts wholesaler and purchase one or two five litre cans of TFR — traffic film remover. Comma and DEB Chemicals product names come to mind. Also buy a five litre can of engine degreaser, called amongst other brand names, Hyper Clean and Jiser.

Try to get the Land Rover safely on some strong axle stands, or ramps so as to reach and see more easily underneath. Wearing goggles, suitable clothing and gloves, spend as much time as necessary loosening all the age old hard packed mud and road grime from under the wheel arches, all around the chassis, outriggers, axles, springs and the underside of the engine and gearbox.

After getting yourself into an appalling filthy and wet state, spray neat concentrated TFR using a garden spray or similar unit to all the areas you have cleaned and let it soak in for a few minutes.

Be warned when applying chemicals, wear not only goggles and gloves but also a mouth and nose mask as well, especially if working in a confined space.

By using the lance jet again after allowing the TFR to do it's job of breaking down the grime, the vehicle's underside should start to look newish again. Although several applications may be necessary, you may well resort to making up a 'spatula' of wood to scrape away more stubborn build up.

Now it's to the engine bay.

Lift the bonnet and remove the securing

pin at the bottom of the bonnet stay. Watch you don't short out the battery terminals when lifting this stay clear of it's bottom pivot. In fact, it's not a bad idea at this stage to disconnect the battery earth strap. With help, lift the bonnet clear of the vehicle and lay down with the underside facing upwards so it can be cleaned.

Spray the whole of the engine bay with neat TFR and allow to soak in for a while, then power wash off being careful not to spray water into the air cleaner or engine breather. Several applications may be necessary. Be cleaning the underside of the bonnet at the same time.

Give the whole vehicle a chance to drip dry for a while, then apply neat engine degreaser throughout the engine bay area and underneath especially around the front swivel housings, steering relay, both diff pinions, propshafts, underside of engine and all around the gearbox and transfer case. Again let it soak in to do it's job. This time we are endeavouring to remove all traces of oil and grease from all surfaces.

After power washing again and perhaps one or two more applications, refit the bonnet and clean down both the inside and outside of the Land Rover. You will now be well and truly soaked to the skin, and generally feel the need of a good hot shower! But I can honestly say that you should feel satisfied with a job well done. After all, it's probably the first decent underside and engine bay clean it's had in many years.

Finally, make sure you shovel the rubbish off the drive, give it a good sweep down and wash off as you don't want any of the oil and grease on your tyres or in your clothes when working underneath.

Planning

Before jumping in with both feet to actually start repairing the vehicle whether it be chassis, bodywork, mechanical or electrical it's not a bad idea to plan your work ahead. To create a plan of action you will need to build up a 'report' on the vehicle.

To assist with making this report, friend and business colleague James Tennant, a 4×4 specialist from nearby Okehampton has allowed us to use his full workshop facilities. James will also be carrying out the specialist work.

Prior to a full on-road test we made a thorough check on the vehicle as it has not been used on the road for quite a few months. To get KYJ to James, I used our trailer.

Starting underneath with a service light, a broad grin from James saying "and another crossmember needed, won't be too long before the rear spring hangers collapse too. It's easier to replace this complete section, that's the rear crossmember together with chassis extensions to take inner rear spring hangers."

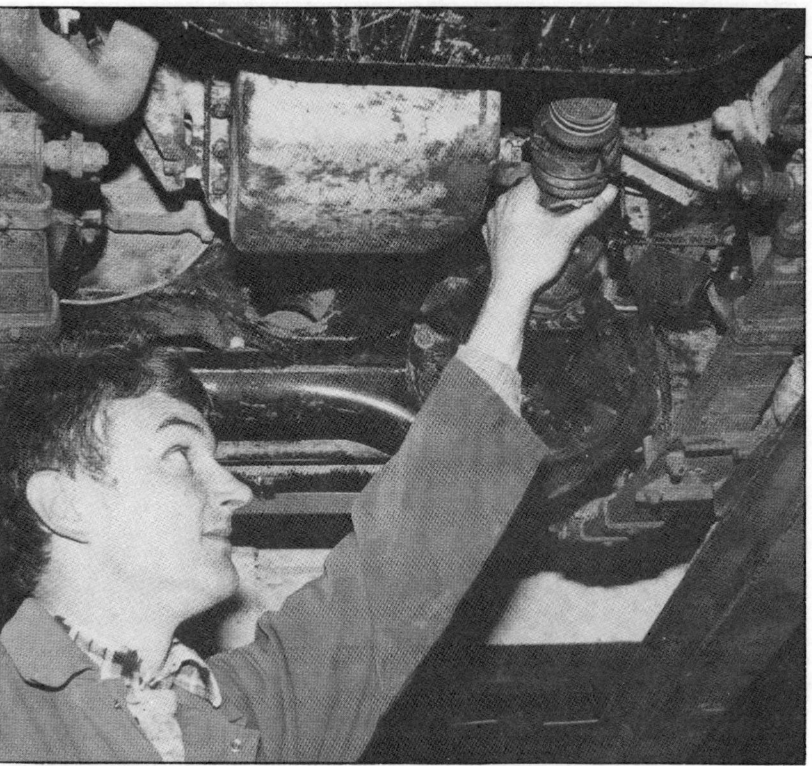

△ *Too much play is felt in the front propshaft. It will be replaced.*

▽ *Checking the gearbox output shaft bearing by lifting the propshaft.*

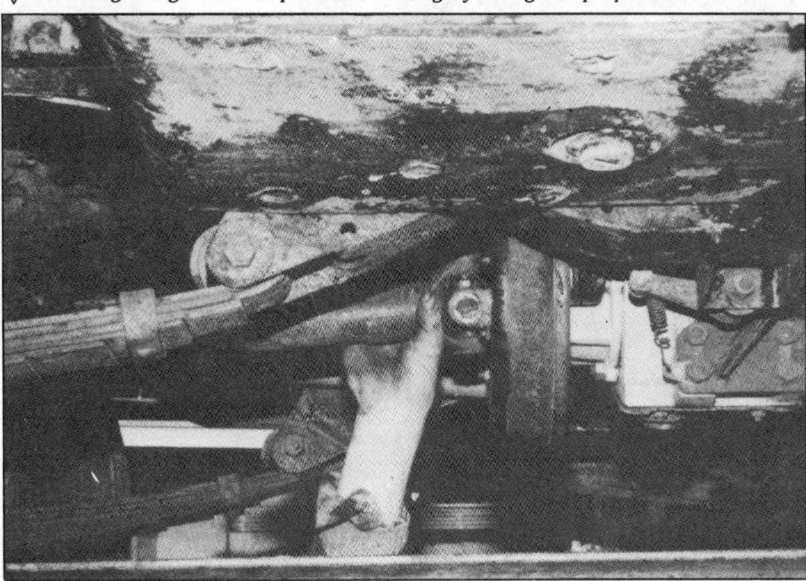

So that's the first main item and as we cast our eyes along under the vehicle we notice a few more nasties.

Plating required to both sides of chassis above rear springs. Both rear body mounting outriggers require replacing, likewise the gearbox crossmember. Front tank outrigger will need renewing, as well as the offside bulkhead outrigger. All these sections are readily available from most parts specialists.

Starting from the front of the vehicle now, we work backwards. The chassis looks much better forward of the bulkhead including the front dumb irons to which the bumper fixes.

James, now satisfied that all the chassis has been checked for corrosion, puts down his welding hammer and reaches for a pry bar to check the various suspension bushes. All are worn by varying degrees and in one case a shackle hole has been elongated. We will come back to the springs later after a test drive as they are looking rather 'flat'. Some wear is evident in the shock absorber rubbers. One bump stop needs replacing.

The front propshaft is completely shot and will require replacement. Nearside gearbox mounting is broken, presumably caused when the crossmember to which it is attached hit something rather solid. The speedo cable is wrongly routed as it enters the gearbox. High/low range level pivot point is badly worn which no doubt will cause much rattling to it's lever in the cab.

Much movement is evident on the handbrake drum which will require further investigation. Not only has the rear

△ *The high/low pivot point shows signs of much wear.*

▽ *Checking the shock absorber bushes by twisting the unit.*

propshaft been fitted back to front but there is some slack on the spline and movement on the U.J.'s. If funds allow we might replace the whole unit. The gearbox output oil seal will have to be replaced as well, likewise the rear axle pinion seal.

The shield of the offside rear shock absorber is well past it and the unit will have to be renewed. Generally the exhaust system looks quite good, although the silencer may not last too much longer and it's adjoining rear bracket is a typical bodge up and requires renewing. We will probably replace the centre mounting too whilst we are at it.

It looks as if the brake pipes have been replaced at some time, probably about two years ago. They have been fitted poorly, but there is no corrosion, so we will just tidy them up and resecure to the chassis. The flexible hoses seem fine.

With me gently moving the steering wheel from side to side, James checks for wear in all the track rod ends. None need replacing, but there is a definite tight spot somewhere in the system, could be either the steering relay or over adjusted swivel pins. Whilst on the subject of swivel housings we might just get away without replacing them as the surface corrosion is not too bad. We might however replace the seals.

Finally, before going out for a test drive, James checks for play in all the wheel bearings by placing his hands firstly each side of each wheel and secondly top and bottom of each wheel, and shakes them. Both back wheels seem fine, but both front bearings will need replacing we think.

After a quick cup of coffee and some of Melanie's home made biscuits it's off for a test drive. James first checks the brakes, whilst I check all the lights and off we go. She pulls up quite nicely, gear changes are smooth, the high/low lever chattering to itself. There are no undue whines from the diffs, gearbox or transfer case. James is impressed. He remarks, "Once we've sorted the chassis out and attended to those main items, we will pick up anything else on a full 24,000 mile service. This should make a nice vehicle when resprayed."

After making sure during the course of a few miles that there is no tendency to jump out of gear or anything else odd, it's back to the workshop. A quick look again underneath confirms traces of oil escaping from where we thought — that's the beauty of power washing the underside before these thorough checks.

Up with the bonnet and all looks remarkably fine. In fact we think the engine could well be a replacement as not only has the whole engine been sprayed over with light green paint, but also there is a rocker oil filler on top as well as a side filler. I must admit that it didn't dawn on me to check the log sheet engine number against the block itself. On Series Ones it is second nature to me!

Looking around the outside of the vehicle we have the following items to replace. Inner wing mudshields both sides and the steering box cover, likewise the offside outer wing and adjoining front headlight panel. We will replace the broken and missing wing mirrors with the door variety. Both the plastic bonnet hinge sockets were missing.

I think the finished vehicle will be worthy of having two replacement windscreen glasses as both show wiper scars. It is our intention to install rear side windows in the coming weeks. A pair of new rear mud flaps won't go amiss either especially as one side is missing anyway. The broken side steps will be removed altogether and the rear step repaired.

A thorough check of the door tops behind the home made trim reveals no problems, so all we need do is replace the glass channels.

I'm still not happy with the road springs and looking from the back she is definitely listing to one side. I think she is also sitting rather low on her flattened springs. If I can get a full set of springs at the right price we might well change them.

After spraying her, she will deserve a nice new set of front seats with matching door trim and perhaps a carpet set.

Well, that's my report, basically a reminder of what work we have to carry out and what major spares are required. The 24,000 mile service will, of course, require a number of service items which will no doubt include new brake shoes all round.

We will carry out the work roughly in the order of this report.

Well I've timed that right, here comes the delivery driver with those chassis sections.

Part Four By David Bowyer

KYJ's chassis, fully repaired, awaits wire-brushing and a coat of protective paint.

Cut out the rot

HAVING RECEIVED the chassis sections, we first made sure that the right ones had arrived before getting the cutting torch out. All the sections that we needed came from PWB at Budbrooke Road, Warwick, who are long standing manufacturers of replacement Land Rover and Range Rover chassis sections and body panels.

A phone call to their very helpful Mr Tim Pickering produced all the information I originally required to find out what was available for KYJ. He explained that all of their products are supplied solely to a large network of dealers and parts outlets spread evenly across the British Isles.

He suggested that we order our requirements from our Land Rover repair specialist, and in our case the nearest company to us was James Tennant from Okehampton. Now isn't life full of surprises. James, of course, is carrying out much of the specialists work.

James and I laid the sections out on the ground facing appropriately either left or right on an 'imitation' chassis and, having ascertained all was there, after a quick brew up in the workshop, we were finally ready to start.

The first most obvious section to replace was the rear cross member. Having driven KYJ onto the ramps, the battery and alternator were disconnected. Two reasons, of course, a lot of loose wires were about to start appearing and secondly, stick or mig welding can seriously damage the health of the vehicle's alternator. It's the diodes in the alternator's internal control that cops it.

We also drained carefully and removed the fuel tank at this stage as both the outriggers supporting it were going to be replaced the following day. Typical, just as we were removing the tank, we noticed a weep from one of the seams. The seam had obviously given up through dislodging the tank. That's something else we are going to need to finish the vehicle. All the carpet and rubber matting was also removed from the vehicle to reduce the possible fire hazard through welding.

Back to the rear cross member, before unbolting some of the ten body mounting bolts along the back of the vehicle we had to support the chassis above the axle safely with blocks of wood under the bump stops. The rear road wheels and exhaust silencer were also removed to gain working space.

△ *Both chassis and axle must be safely supported before cutting off the complete rear cross member*

The new gearbox cross member securely welded to the chassis, replacing its badly damaged predecessor ▷

Finally the wiring loom was moved clear.

The spring bush bolts were then removed with a little careful jacking to release the tension. At this stage the last of the rearmost body bolts stayed in place to support the rotten section whilst cutting it out.

Now this is where the specialist comes in, armed with an oxy-acetylene cutting torch, the whole section is soon cut away from the remainder of the chassis just forward of the rear spring hangers, making sure, of course, that the chassis extensions of the new replacement cross member reached well past the decided point of cutting. With my gloved hands supporting the rotten member, James undid the remaining body bolts and the unit was lifted clear.

After tidying up the cuts on the chassis with the grinderette, a liberal coat of black Hammerite was given. The new cross member was then offered up into position by sliding the extensions over the chassis rails and refitting just two of the body bolts. With a little tapping here and there the new unit soon lined up.

The chassis was well scraped and cleaned up with the grinder where we were about to weld the new to the old. The new extensions were hammered in a little to give a tight fit onto the existing chassis ready for welding.

James then professionally welded the side and underside joints with his Mig welder. The joint across the top of the chassis was welded with a traditional arc welder as the rod has to be curved to reach over the top and under the rear floor area. Obviously if the rear body had been taken off, this wouldn' t have posed a problem.

I know it all sounds so simple in offering up and welding this large new cross member into place, but the beauty is that the replacement is designed and made to fit without too much hassle. The spring bush bolts were then temporarily refitted to the new spring hangers attached to the new unit after some more careful jacking to remove the support blocks above the chassis. We will be fitting a full set of new road springs later.

Next on the agenda was the removal of the offside rear body outrigger which was a simple case of first burning off the two body mounting bolts with the oxy-acetylene torch and then cutting the then free outrigger flush off the chassis. With the torch still in hand, the body mounting plate was

△ *The replacement outriggers have base plates to facilitate easy positioning and welding to the chassis*

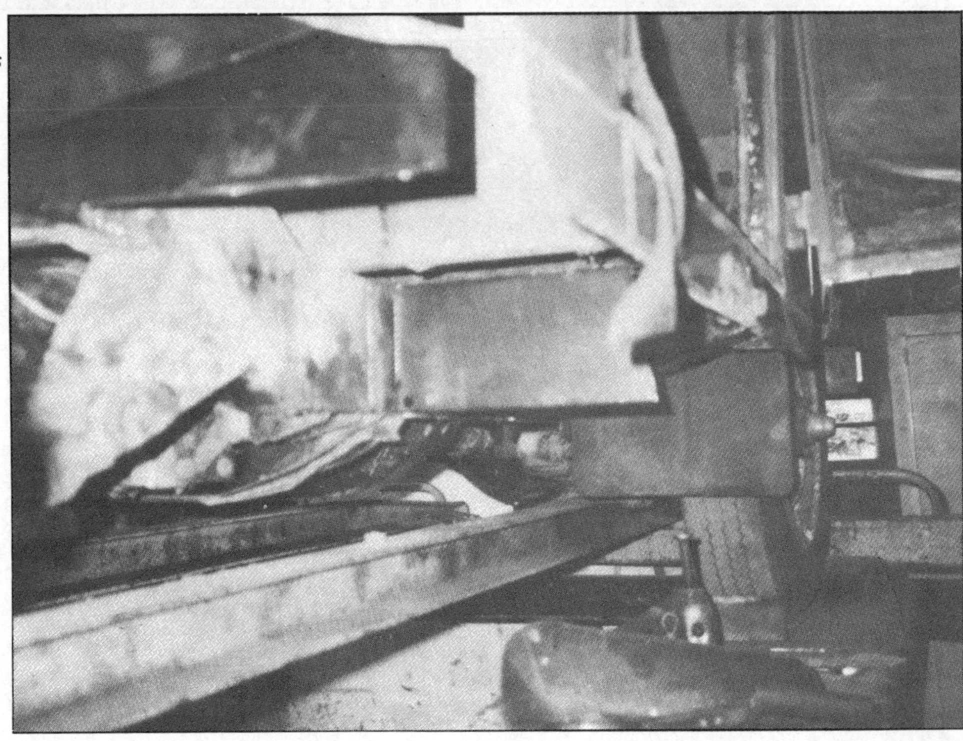

The two tank outriggers neatly welded into place. We will paint the chassis before replacing the fuel tank ▷

cut off the outrigger for welding back onto the new one. The front tank outrigger was then also cut off in a similar manner, but only after undoing the bolts and screws holding down the driver's floor panel to gain access from above.

And whilst working on this side we removed the bolt securing the existing bulkhead outrigger to the bodywork. Glad we sprayed the threads with WD40 beforehand! We had to support the bulkhead a touch with a bottle jack and a block of wood. The old outrigger was then cut off in a similar fashion like the others.

All these replacement outriggers come equipped with a chassis plate to make welding them onto the chassis as easy as possible as can be seen from the photographs. But in each case the chassis must be ground back flush to accept these plates. You also need to make sure that there is no paint or rust where you go to weld. It's best to use the grinderette to clean the surface up.

Fortunately we remembered to take the measurements between the two tank mounting outriggers to know the final position for both of them to be welded into place. The rear body replacement unit was held up in place alongside the body mounting plate (this was cut off the old outrigger and bolted back) and the unit squared up before tack welding into place. With James happy at that, he mig welded it fully into place. He finally welded the body mounting plate onto the outrigger.

Next followed the front tank outrigger holding it into place with a carver cramp onto the chassis. When we were happy with it's positioning in relation to it's sister tank/body outrigger, it was finally welded onto the chassis. We did, in fact, lift the tank up into position to check it fitted into place first. The bulkhead outrigger was offered up next and is attached to the bulkhead with it's original nut and bolt. It's opposite end is clamped against the chassis with the carver cramp and tapped squarely into place, and finally welded.

We made an early start the following morning starting with the removal of the rear nearside body outrigger. It does not take long. This time I used the mig welder, bringing back memories of using college migs and tigs at evening classes.

The next task was the replacement of the twisted and split gearbox cross mem-

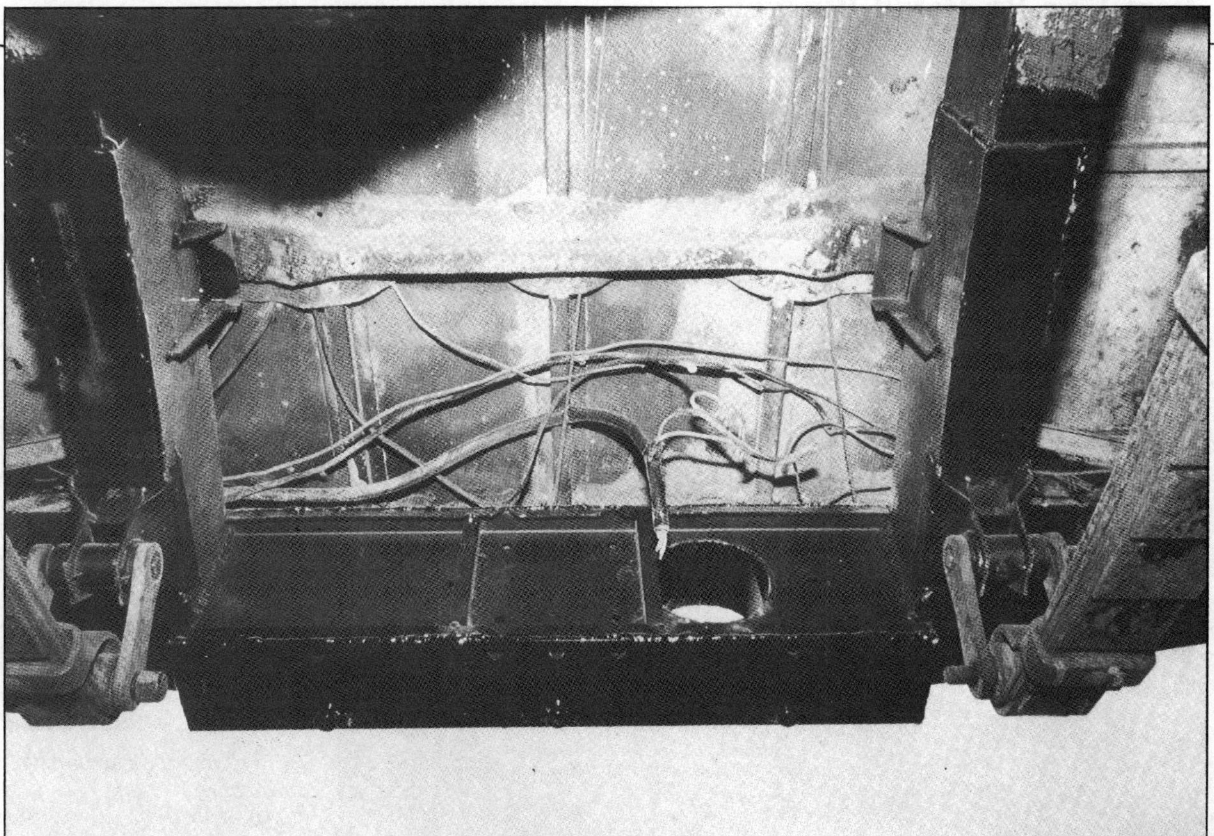

△ *The new cross member with its chassis extensions and spring hangers*

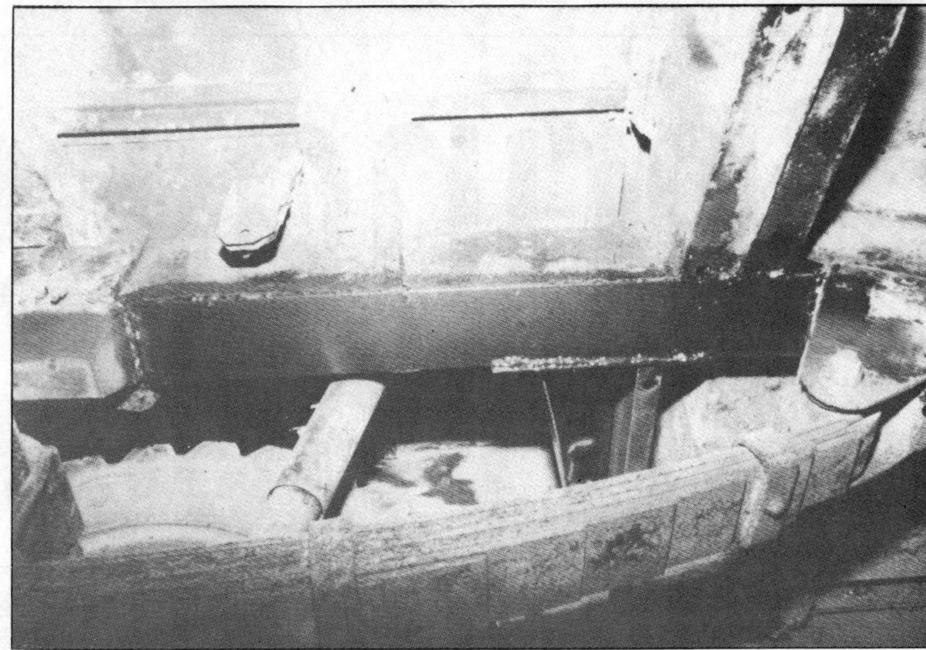

A strip of steel, the same thickness as the chassis, is used to plate the badly rotted areas above the rear springs ▷

ber. First job was to support the gearbox. remove the mounting bushes and replace with a matching set. James then used the oxy-acetylene torch to remove the still fixed end of the cross member. That out of the way I cleaned the chassis up with the angle grinder ready to receive the replacement unit.

We lined it up onto the new bushes to give it's position, then clamped it to the underside of the chassis. Again I welded the PWB cross member into place. With the gearbox fully lowered back into place the bush nuts were tightened.

And so we had nearly finished the chassis work. After lunch James cut to length two strips of metal to weld onto the underside of each chassis rail between the bump stops and the spring hangers above the rear springs. These were then bent to shape of the chassis until they were a good fit.

The brake pipe was eased away from the chassis and I used the grinderette to remove the surface rust along the bottom edges of the chassis where we were to weld. Then, in turn, the formed plates were clamped up into position for James to weld securely to the chassis.

All that was left to do that day was finally to check all over the remainder of the chassis in case anything else needed attending to. Fortunately nothing did. I then cleaned up all the welds with the grinderette and painted them and the plates we had just made with smooth black Hammerite to give an initial protection.

Sometime during the next few weeks we shall finish wire brushing down the remaining untouched parts of the chassis and give the whole lot two or three coats of Hammerite to give a long lasting protection. I shall also be applying Waxoyl to the whole of the inside of the chassis.

As always, when working on a vehicle in a workshop, especially when cutting, grinding and welding, protective overalls and leather shoes must always be worn. Likewise the appropriate goggles and masks are used as second nature, and a fire extinguisher must be handy.

My thanks to James Tennant for his professional services and use of his facilities. He can be contacted at his workshop near Okehampton, Tel: (0837) 86478.

Also my thanks to Tim Pickering of PWB, Tel: (0926) 494782.

Part Five By David Bowyer

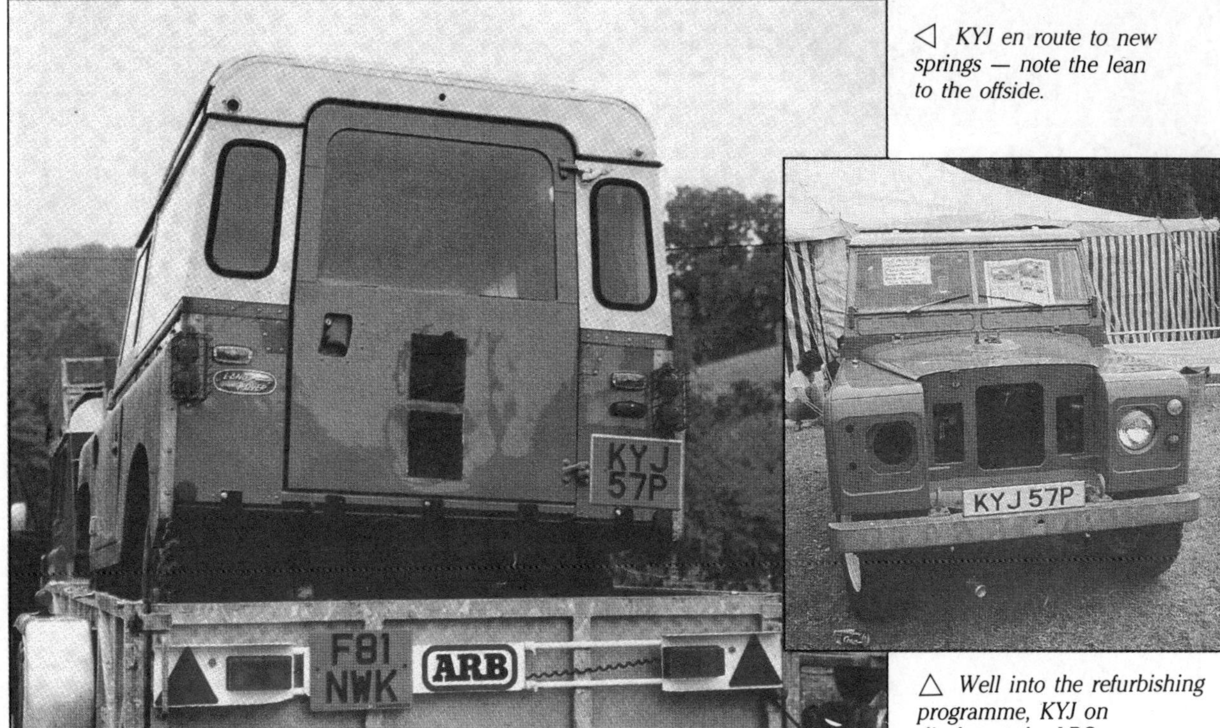

◁ *KYJ en route to new springs — note the lean to the offside.*

△ *Well into the refurbishing programme, KYJ on display at the LRO Billing rally.*

Springing into action

SERIES III PROJECT

IT'S BEEN a busy few weeks recently in carrying on with the various types of repair, replacement and refurbishment works of our project vehicle. This sudden concentration of effort was largely brought about through needing a presentable vehicle for display at LRO's Family Off Road Weekend staged over the last two days of June.

And I must admit that, "she" did look good in the central arena, all spick and span in her new coat of paint. Many visitors to the event showed their appreciation by way of nice comments, and I was amazed to see so many readers getting down on their hands and knees and having a 'good look' underneath her.

It is with grateful thanks to James Tennant and his apprentice, Darren Phare, for providing the full facilities for continuing the mechanical works, and David Knight for preparing and spraying KYJ in a make-shift spraybooth in my own workshop at our Centre.

In preparation for LRO's event, between us, we carried out the following work. Replaced the offside outer wing and head-light panel, prepared, staightened and filled the many small dents, primed and re-sprayed the outside of the vehicle.

I stripped out most of the old interior panel cladding together with sundry brackets to do with it's previous caravanette conversion, chucked out the old front seats, dug out, quite literally, all the accumulated hay, straw and rubbish from the parcel shelf, behind and under the seats, finishing with giving the whole inside it's first scrub out.

It was really filfthy!

After all that, I popped KYJ back onto the trailer to take her to James' workshop. First we prepared and installed the new fuel tank, fitted four new springs, sorted out the exhaust system, repaired the Fairey over-drive lever, fitted a new bump stop, primed and painted the floor plates and footwells, trimmed the bulkhead, gearbox tunnel, floor and seatbox with carpet. Finally a set of county style cloth front seats were fitted into position.

Now, of course, most of this work has been carried out in completely the wrong order, but it was nice to present her well at the LRO weekend and certainly gave me a boost to get on with the work.

Anyway, back to the work in hand, let's take a look at changing the road springs and shock absorbers in this issue. We can follow the rest of the work mentioned sooner or later.

The appropriate road springs arrived at very short notice from PWB Warwick having negotiated a very keen price. Having checked that the correct ones were sent (of course we were sent the right ones,

◁ *Darren working hard to undo the "U" bolts.*

A sharp thump dislodges the spring from its locating ▽ *peg and hole.*

◁ *The metal support is lowered on the trolley jack to relieve the tension on the spring.*

how silly of me) as each spring bares a different number.

The driver's side and the passenger's side must not be interchanged. A stiffer spring is fitted to the driver's side.

Springs can be identified by the increased camber of the spring fitted to the driver's side and by the part number stamped on the underside of the third leaf. We also made sure before starting the work that sufficient new "U" bolts and shackle plates were in stock in case they were required, as well as new self locking nylon nuts for the "U" bolts, spring bush and shackle bolts. Never re-use old self locking nuts on any steering, suspension or braking system.

Firstly we drove KYJ up onto James' 4-post ramp and chocked both wheels opposite the end we are working on. At this stage we still had the fuel tank missing so I had to dump the fuel lift pipe into my spare fuel can. The can was then removed from the vehicle.

In turn we tackled one spring at a time loosening the four "U" bolt nuts having firstly sprayed the protruding threads with WD40. We also undid the bottom of the shock absorbers.

When undoing nuts from protruding threads don't be tempted to rush things, like using long levers to hurry things up. If you do, you could soon start shearing studs. The best way is to wire brush any rust out of the threads and apply more WD40. Make sure you use the right sized socket and gently and firmly try undoing it.

If you are lucky enough to undo a turn or two before the nut tightens again on the exposed thread, spray some more oil above the nut, retighten, spray more oil below and undo the nut again. By moving the nut backwards and forwards along the thread in this fashion you could well save the "U" bolts.

If, on the other hand, the threads are damaged by clouting the ground once too often then it's out with the oxy-acetylene torch. Thank you James for coming to the rescue as the rear spring "U" bolt nuts definitely needed cutting off.

Before undoing any nuts too far, it's very important to support the chassis with an appropriate stout piece of wood. A six foot length, by three inches square is perfect. The vehicle was then lowered onto this support. A second support was cut to length from some hollow square tubing which was used to hold up the bottom plate through which the "U" bolt threads protrude. This support is raised into place by lifting on a trolley jack.

This second support is as equally important as the first. Start by raising to just supporting the axle, then finish removing the four "U" bolt nuts. Then, with one hand holding the upright, give a sharp blow to

◁ *Tightening up the bush bolts using a ¾" drive socket and a bit of grunt!*

James carefully easing a spring over with a bar to locate its peg into the hole under the axle. His eyes glance across the axle to make sure all is well. ▷

◁ *Daren tightens the "U" bolt nuts using a ½" drive socket.*

the top of the old spring in order to break it clear from the axle. Think out what you are doing because the sudden releasing of the spring from the axle will make you jump, if unprepared.

Now check the spring hanger bracket bush by loosening the top nut, followed by the bolt itself just a turn or two to see if any wear is present by using a lever. We were lucky as in each case on the front these bushes were OK. On the back of the vehicle new bushes were supplied and ready fitted on the rear cross member chassis extensions.

Next stage is to remove the spring itself. A ¾" drive socket is ideal for this with an appropriate ring spanner to hold the bolt head. Undo the front nut first, then the bottom shackle bolt nut. Following the removal of this nut, unscrew the bolt itself from the inner threaded shackle plate.

Have someone take the weight of the spring as the bolt is driven clear out of the bush. Let the spring hinge down on it's loose front fixing and drive the bolt out with a drift. Move the old spring well clear of the vehicle as you don't want to trip over it.

Now take out the top shackle bolt for inspection. Before attempting to fit the replacement new spring, check and clean the three bolts, and if you are not happy with them — replace them with new.

Check also the shackles themselves. If there is any sign of wear in either of the clear or threaded holes, change them for new. The same applies to the two "U" bolts, if they are in perfect condition by all means use them again, if not, replace.

As I've said before, you are not using any existing nuts as they are all being replaced with new Nyloc nuts. But make sure you have the right size and pitch of nut threads to suit the new or existing bolts. If you are only changing one of the shackle plates make sure that the replacement has identical hole centres.

Right, Darren and I are now ready to hang into position the new spring. Once again we check that we have the right part number for the right corner of the vehicle. We hang it on the front bolt first, then hinge it upwards so as to knock the bottom shackle bolt through the spring bush. The threaded shackle plate is then offered up and both the top and bottom bolts are screwed up into position, but not tightly at this stage.

The metal support is then brought back into play by jacking it up under the bottom plate. The plate is manoeuvred so the "U" bolt holes are equal each side of the new spring. As the jack is raised the spring is slightly prized sideways with another bar in order to align the peg in the middle of the top of the spring with it's mating hole under the axle. Make sure at all times during this operation that your wooden support stays firmly and safely under the chassis cross member.

With the axle supported and ▷ the road wheel removed, it's easy to change the shock absorbers.

▽ Turning over the new split pin ends with a stout pair of pliers locating a bottom shock absorber bush. We will be hacksawing off those protruding "U" bolt studs.

KYJ sitting nice and level on ▷ her new springs all ready for the Billing Show.

When all is lined up drop the "U" bolts down over the axle and through the bottom plates, and fit the new Nylocs and partly tighten. Before the final tightening up of all the nuts (on each side of each axle) jump up into the vehicle and bounce it up and down to settle the angle of the spring shackles.

The shackle bolts which clamp the hanger bracket bushes must not be tightened until the spring is positioned in the mid-point of it's deflection range. This ensures that excessive rotation/shear forces are not imparted to the bush, centres. Failure to observe this instruction can adversely affect bush life, especially in off-road conditions which produces large spring deflections. The workshop manual gives you the correct dimensions.

Finally, fully tighten all the nuts. As a guide, use ½" drive socket to tighten the "U" bolt nuts as tight as you can, and on the bush and shackle bolts use a ¾" drive socket and do the same again. Don't forget to tighten up the shackle bolts first into the threaded holes of the inner plates before tightening the nuts on the same bolts.

The procedure for replacing all four springs is identical. You will find that the "U" bolts on each axle being right next to the diff itself are slightly longer and if any of the threads protrude more than two or three threads through the nut then hacksaw the surplus off.

Darren and I replaced three of the springs before lunch leaving one for after. Which just goes to show, if you have the items to hand and a hoist to place the vehicle on, changing springs is not too long a job.

Having 're-sprung' the vehicle so to speak, we finished off the day by sorting out the exhaust system (more of that later) and checking the shock absorbers. In my report, you will remember, we reckoned to change two of them. Sure enough we replaced those two. On checking the third it was noticed that the bottom 'eye' was parting company with the unit itself. As we have gone this far, and as when changing shock absorbers they must always be changed in axle sets, you've guessed it, KYJ is sitting on four new springs with matching new shocks. And as most of the bushes were worn they have also been replaced.

To change the shock absorbers, simply support the axle under the spring, remove the road wheel, straighten out the split pin holding the washer over the bottom outer bush and yank it out — discard it. Undo the chassis nut and bolt supporting the top bush and remove the unit altogether. We of course undid the bottom of the shock absorbers and hinged them up and out of the way before changing the springs.

To test the unit, put one eye into the bench vice and lift the other end up vertically. It should expand evenly showing no sign of tightness or slackness at any point, (there is a greater resistance on the extension stroke) and the same goes for when compressing the unit. Move the piston in and out fully several times. If it doesn't run evenly both ways then discard it.

Refitting couldn't be easier. Place the top bolt through the washer and bushes each side of the eye, and as you push the bolt through the chassis, place the bottom eye over the bush next to the spring. Place the bottom bush over it's support along with it's washer.

Tighten a pair of Molegrips over the support against the washer with the opening of the jaw giving a clearance to the split pin hole. Tap the Molegrips sideways until you can drop a new splitpin through. Turn over the protruding ends with the pliers and finish tightening the top nut and bolt. They say you learn something new every day.

Throughout the whole operation if the work is new to you, keep referring to that workshop manual as it would save you much time and frustration. Be sure too, to double check the tightness of all the major nuts and bolts by using a torque wrench set in accordance with the manual.

Part six by David Bowyer

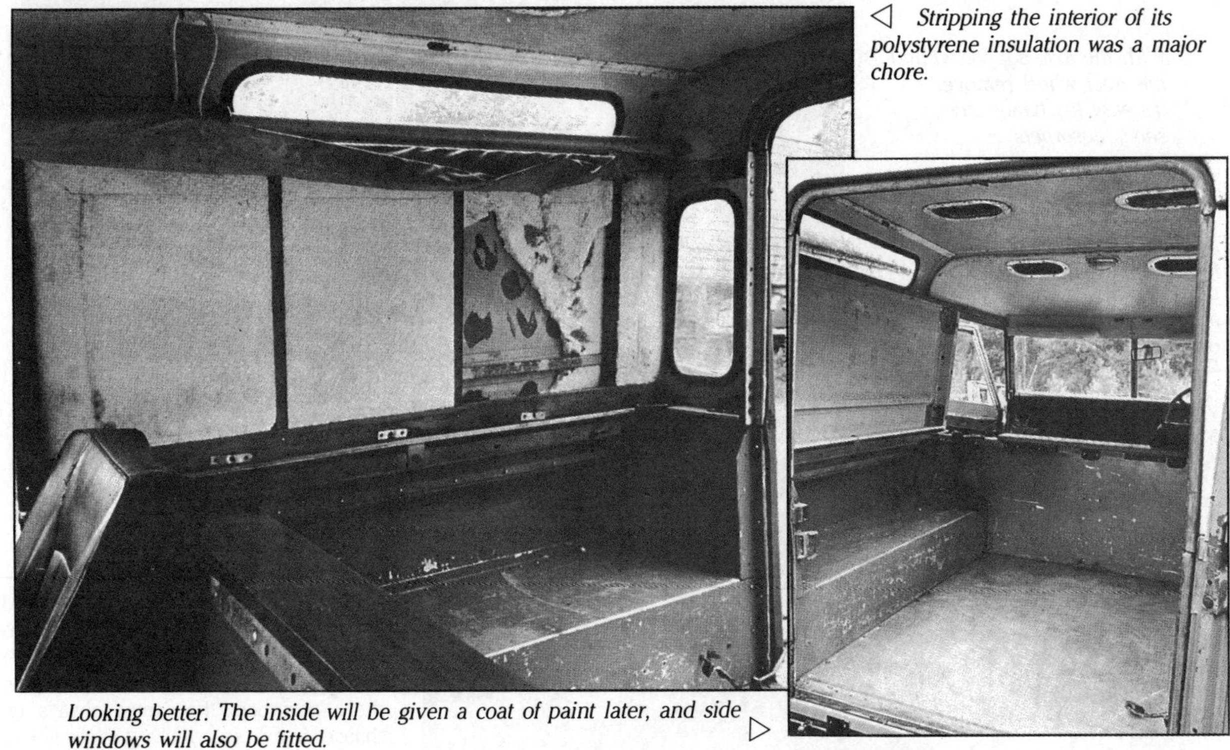

◁ *Stripping the interior of its polystyrene insulation was a major chore.*

Looking better. The inside will be given a coat of paint later, and side windows will also be fitted. ▷

The clean up begins

WE CONTINUE this month by catching up with many of those odd jobs prior to chassis painting, a full service and my next article which will cover respraying.

You will remember I told you how filthy the vehicle was inside, well the rubbish wasn't only many years of straw and hay inside. It was also the mess I made when removing the old home made inside cladding, top side rails and various bits and bobs to do with her being used as a camper.

The rails inside supported slide-out tubes to hang an external tent on, but as the latter is missing I have no idea how it all came together. If a reader out there knows of this vehicle, a phone call would be appreciated.

Whoever carried out the internal cladding and fitting of the tubes, clips and covers, certainly made a super job of it. Although I've taken it all out, I'm saving it, as whoever eventually takes care of KYJ is most welcome to these items.

Having prized out the two thicknesses of polystyrene sheeting between the framework, I had one hell of a game in getting the old cement or glue or whatever it was off the panels. It was a question of simply having patience and scraping off with a one inch scraper a little at a time. The framework itself, which was very professionally jointed, must have been made by either a very competent DIY person or a joiner.

After cleaning out the vehicle I took the opportunity of washing the whole of the inside to remove much grime that had obviously built up over the years. When we eventually complete the vehicle I shall use proprietary cleaners and polishes, but in this first instance I simply used Jiff, a sponge and buckets of warm water to clean the whole of the inside. And doing that was most satisfying.

Back down at James's workshop the original petrol tank was stripped of its sender unit and petrol pick up pipe in readiness to be fitted to the new tank. As well as new gaskets being used, Blue Hylomar jointing compound is always used as well to make 'perfect' joints. Prior to installing the new tank, masking tape was applied to the inlet, breather tube, outlet and terminals on the sender unit to allow

△ *The old, leaking, fuel tank is discarded, while the replacement has been coated in underseal, ready to receive fuel pipes and sender unit.*

"County" cloth seats are replacing the worn out vinyl originals. ▷

for the top and sides to be sprayed with a good coating of vehicle underseal. The underside will be done similarly about the time of chassis painting.

Fitting the new tank was easy enough, lift up into position and hold into place on a bottle jack, and loosely fit the front new 6mm bolts and washers. The back of the tank should only have one bolt and bush set in the centre hole to save strain on the tank should there be any flexing between the tank outriggers.

Tighten up all four bolts, reconnect the large diameter supply hose from the fuel filler, refit the breather pipe, union to petrol pick up pipe and finally the sender unit terminals. Don't forget to check the tightness of the drain plug onto it's sealing washer. Fill the tank with some new clean petrol, reconnect the battery and run the engine for a moment or two to make sure all is well.

Here comes another warning again. When changing tanks, NEVER drain petrol from a vehicle standing over a pit. Petrol vapour is highly inflammable, and in confined spaces is also very explosive and toxic. Drain only outside the workshop where there can be no fear of ignition through nearby leadlamps, etc.

The exhaust system is the next item on the agenda. There is only the existing front downpipe in position at this stage and that's hanging loose. We unbolt it from the manifold to check the joint as I remember that there was a fair old exhaust blow from this area before we started work on KYJ.

You must be very very careful when undoing the three nuts holding this joint up underneath the exhaust manifold. Use only a ⅜" drive socket set with a long extension to reach up beside the downpipe and only after spraying WD40 up there. Get the nuts moving backwards and forwards as you slowly undo.

Any rushing, or applying too much strain, will simply shear the studs protruding from the manifold. If you are unlucky to have this happen like it has happened to me before now, the manifold would have to come off to have new studs fitted.

Having got the downpipe off it was easy to see why we had an exhaust blow. The ▷

△ *Be careful not to use too much pressure on the ⅜" socket set when tightening up the manifold nuts.*

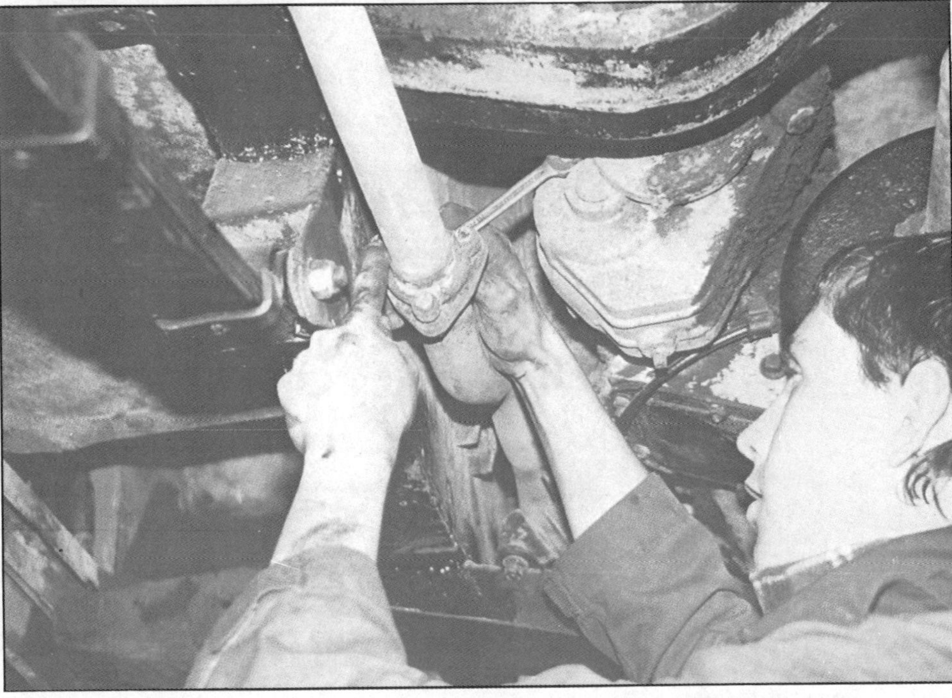

◁ *Assembling the joint between the intermediate and front exhaust pipes. Tighten up the nuts equally.*

metal olive had nearly parted company with the pipe itself. No problem, after wire brushing and taping back into place, the olive was mig welded securely to the pipe. Before refitting the pipe Darren cleaned up the welding with the grinderette.

When either replacing or refitting an entire exhaust system, start with the front pipe first, loosely tightening the manifold nuts using Copperease grease on the studs first. Then check the condition and replace items as required of the two chassis mounted exhaust saddles, one being half way along the intermediate pipe, the other attaches to the tail pipe.

If starting with a bag of new bits, follow the instructions in either the parts or workshop manual for order of assembly.

The intermediate pipe is then offered up and loosely connected to it's mating joint to the front pipe, making sure the joint is clean, of course. Also loosely secure the saddle of the hanging bracket.

Hang up into position the silencer and tail pipe using a new copper gasket to joint it to the intermediate pipe and again loosely secure the saddle of the rearmost hanging bracket.

Finally, adjust the whole system to hang properly with the two hanging brackets pointing down vertically. Make sure, too, that the front and intermediate pipes run parallel to the main chassis rail with sufficient space between, likewise the pipes must be well clear of the middle cross member and gearbox mounting.

Start by tightening the manifold nuts at the front and work through to the back of the system, using just sufficient pressure as necessary, especially the manifold nuts. Use all new nuts, bolts and spring washers for this final assembly. Start the engine and make sure the system is still well clear of the chassis when blipping the throttle. Your pride and joy should now sound sweeter!

Whilst working under the vehicle we took the opportunity of replacing the missing "bump stop", by simply undoing the bolts each side of the chassis, discarding the broken part and replacing with a new one using new bolts and nuts. The bump

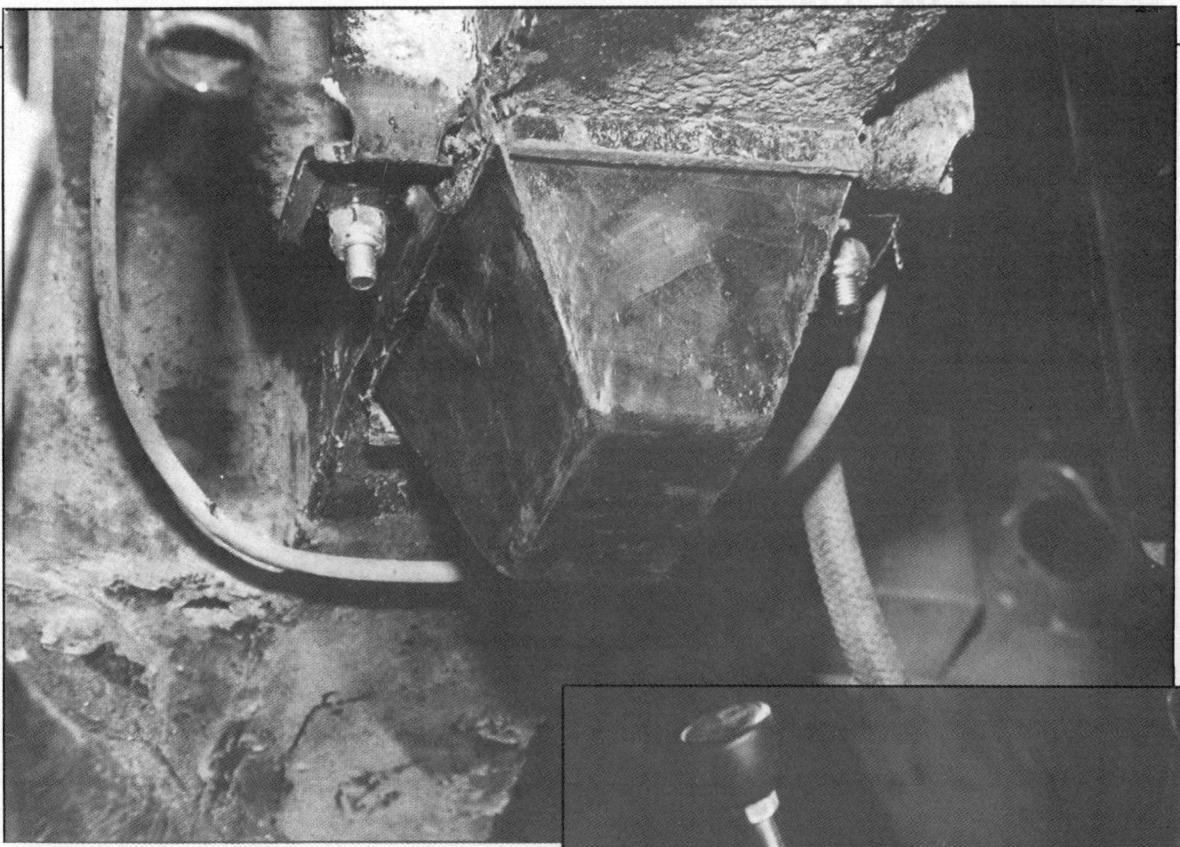

△ *The new bump stop installed on the chassis above the axle.*

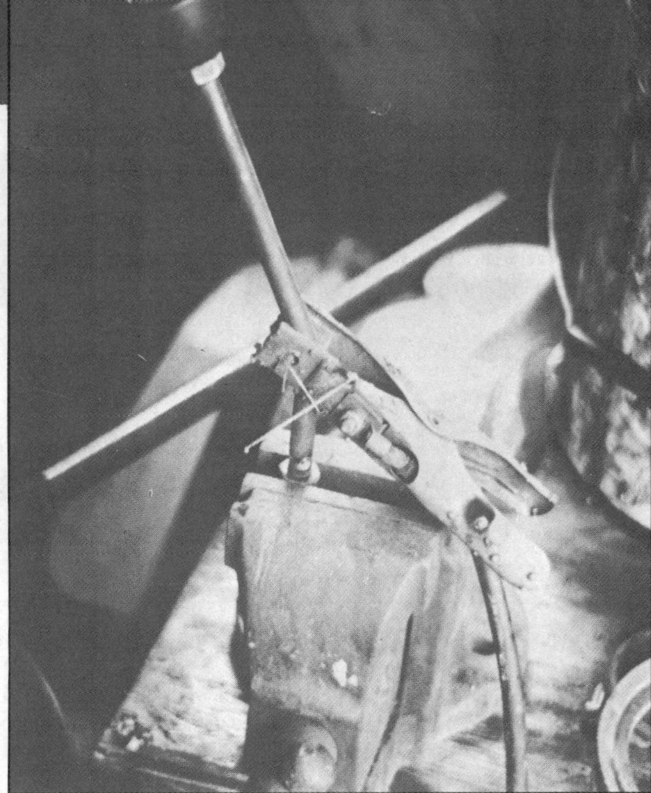

The snapped off overdrive lever is welded back together. ▷

stops are fitted under the chassis directly above each end of each axle simply to stop the chassis from hitting the axle when the wheel on that side is pushed hard up into the wheelarch when getting cross axled, for instance.

You will remember me telling you that the Fairey Overdrive operating lever was loose in the parcel shelf when the vehicle was bought. Well I thought now is the time to see if we could repair it by welding the snapped off end back on to it's stud protruding from the unit itself.

First I wanted to establish why the lever had broken in the first place. The pivot on which the lever was attached was seized onto it's pivot bolt. All that was needed to remedy the situation was simply some cleaning of the assembly and a smear of fresh oil on the pivot bolt.

It's a pity that the previous owner didn't realise that something was amiss when the lever got stiffer to operate, and did something about it, rather than force the lever and break it. Still we are all human aren't we!

As can be seen from the photo, the lower part was secured in the vice by its nut, with the lever held above with the welding earth clamp — it's earth clamp being pinched in the vice. With the two ends chamfered off on the grindstone first, the lever is brought back to life with the mig welder.

We finished the day off by attaching the trade plates to go and fill up with petrol and carry out a road test to satisfy ourselves all the work carried out recently is working correctly.

Next month I will cover the replacing of the wing panel, preparation and respraying of KYJ.

Part seven by David Bowyer

◁ *After the minor dents are beaten out and cleaned back, bodyfiller is applied.*

Painting your wagon

THE MOST satisfying part of any refurbishment of a vehicle has surely got to be the completion of respraying the bodywork. In a matter of a few hours once all the preparation and masking is completed you can soon bring the vehicle back to it's former glory. As the adverts so often say, 'it looks like new'.

Although KYJ seemed in reasonable shape when we bought her, on closer inspection prior to preparing to start tidying up the bodywork, there were more blemishes than we thought. Fortunately, the only major replacement of panels was the outer offside wing and matching front headlight panel and box behind.

These panels were supplied by James Tennant and manufactured by PWB Replacement Motor Parts Ltd. of Warwick — the company who supplied the chassis sections. The various pop rivets were drilled out and the existing bolts undone after a good soaking in WD40. In no time at all we had these panels secured in place with new fixings.

At this stage the three doors had their hinges reset so they closed more squarely and whilst at it, the door keep plates were adjusted. It is always a good idea to carry out this work before commencing respraying.

From here on, all the rest of the preparation and spraying was carried out by David Knight a professional Auto Refinisher from Buckinghamshire. David, who is often down at our Off Road Centre with his Range Rover expressed an interest in our project vehicle when we first bought her.

He arrived on the Friday night of the three day May Bank Holiday. This doubled up with James Tennant fitting Air Lockers on his Range Rover, so as David was left without a vehicle, this gave him an ideal opportunity of working on the Series III.

As it was a fine sunny weekend, David carried out much of the preparation work out in the yard. First the bonnet was removed to make it easier to work on. The various odd pieces of trim were removed to a safe place. Then each panel, one by one was carefully rubbed down and minor dents beaten out using a hammer and dolly. The affected areas were then sanded over to blend the repairs in with the surrounding bodywork using 80 grit sandpaper to give a good key for the bodyfiller.

Straightening out the lips around the edge of the outer skin of the roof was accomplished with the aid of a block of wood and hammering carefully the lip square to the top. Mole grips are useful too.

David used Plastic Padding PP50 bodyfiller to fill and finish off all the reshaped and repaired areas. When hardened off this was sanded back and roughly feathered to blend into the surrounding paintwork with 80 grit using a hand sanding block.

A paint scraper was used to remove all loose and flaking paint found on previous repairs around the vehicle. Also around the edges of panels and windows in internal corners and gutter areas.

180 grit discs on an air powered Dual

◁ *Repaired and filled areas being sanded down by hand.*

An air-powered sander being used to "feather-edge" the repaired areas ▷

Action sander was then used to 'feather-edge' all the repaired areas and where the loose paint had been scraped off. This was followed by brushing 2 pack 'Extra-Filler primer' over all the repaired areas quickly followed by two more coats using 4 parts primer to 1 part Express Hardner.

Immediately after applying these three coats directly over these primed areas, a lightly sprayed 'guide coat' of green aerosol (any dark colour will do) to highlight scratches, high spots and low spots when wet sanding.

The primer was allowed to fully harden and shrink over the Saturday night. The following morning all the primed areas were wet sanded with 400 grit 'wet and dry' paper using a hand sanding block. This was followed by wet sanding the entire vehicle from top to bottom with 400 'wet and dry', again by hand. Finally KYJ was completely wiped down with a soft damp cloth to remove all the dust, followed by thoroughly drying the vehicle with all it's nooks and crannies with an air blow gun and paper towels.

After Sunday lunch it's time to start masking the windows, door rubbers, galvanised cappings and all the lower areas in preparation to spray the roof and sides. By this stage KYJ had to be driven into the makeshift spray booth in our garage. This 'spray booth' was simply made by securing thin polythene sheeting up to the ceiling joists with a few lengths of 2″ × 1″ batten, leaving the sides draping down to the floor, which was fastened down with weights. Joints in the polythene were sealed with masking tape to prevent overspray getting through and coating everything in sight.

The majority of masking to the original lower blue areas was carried out by using 3 foot brown masking paper, but old newspaper is quite suitable. Care must be taken when applying masking tape, especially around the rubber surrounds to the alpine lights and windows to ensure it is placed accurately. Both 1″ and 2″ widths of tape are normally used.

Areas to be sprayed must first be degreased using special Bodyclean Degreaser to ensure a perfectly clean finish. The workshop floor before this was lightly brushed and dampened with water so as to keep dust down to an absolute minimum. A final blow off with the air gun is made to expell any dust and bits still trapped in the gutters and corners.

The whole area is then 'Tack Ragged' to remove any fine dust and dirt on the surface of the panels. Cleanliness at this stage is crucial if you want to achieve a good paint finish.

Now it's on to the spraying. Best to buy a cheap pair of paper type sprayer's overalls to not only protect you, but even the cleanest overalls trap dust which will ruin your paint finish. And in any case you would never be able to clean them afterwards. Wear also an appropriate charcoal nose and mouth mask.

First spray on two light coats of a 2 pack wet on wet Etch Primer Sealer over the whole area starting with the top and work-

▷

◁ *A lightly sprayed guide coat of dark aerosol is applied to the primed areas.*

Make-shift spray booth. ▷

ing down the sides keeping the gun on the move all the time about 12″ from the surface. The proportions for this primer sealer is 2:1:1 mixing ratio. 2 parts Etch Primer, 1 part Activator and 1 part Thinner. This was then allowed to dry for 20 minutes. After this short drying period the surface was 'de-nibbed' lightly with 1200 wet and dry using no water to remove any imperfections, then carefully wiped over.

The three top coats were then applied using ICI 2 pack mixed at a 4:2:1 ratio using ICI's slowest drying '770' hardner giving the best gloss and flow out ('790' for cold conditions). Each coat was applied a few minutes apart as the weather was so warm early on the Sunday evening. But expect to have to wait up to 20 minutes between coats, if the temperature is cool.

It is better to apply three thinner coats of paint rather than two 'thick' coats. If you are unfortunate enough to get a 'run', use the spray gun to run the paint off the panel by applying more paint and working your way down off the panel allowing gravity to do it's work. Before hardening wipe off drips with a piece of rag at the bottom edge of the panel.

Small runs are best left well alone as they can be blocked out with 1200 wet and dry and finished with a medium — course polishing compound. If all goes wrong on a particular panel, let it harden over two to three hours (don't try and force dry in a couple of minutes with a hot air gun or heater as all you will succeed in doing is blistering the paint and perhaps buckling a panel) and sand back again with 400.

As it's late on Sunday evening after cleaning the spray gun with Gunwash, David sits down to a well deserved meal and a pint.

First thing Monday morning David draws open the garage doors and casts his eyes intently over the fresh limestone and mutters 'looks good'. The brown masking paper and tape is carefully stripped off the vehicle.

All the limestone area is now masked over. The engine bay is covered in masking paper and taped up, likewise the radiator behind the front panel. Also the exposed galvanised cappings, fuel filler, door handles, front bumper, rear cross member and sundry bits and bobs are all neatly taped up. The various apertures are taped up from behind to stop the paint coating behind. Finally the wheels are covered by the brown paper being taped behind.

The bonnet was prepared in a similar fashion with it's hinges and spare wheel mounting suitably protected. The panel was then placed on top of a stack of Land Rover tyres to give a good working height for spraying.

David, having had an early lunch was then ready to carry out the final cleaning preparations prior to spraying the 'blue' areas. First by cleaning the workshop floor again and dampening, applying the Bodyclean Degreaser, blowing out trapped dust and finally Tack Ragging.

The Etch Primer Sealer is mixed and prepared, the gun ready, and spraying commences. The air is still outside so the

◁ *Using the air powered rotary polisher to finish off the medium/course polishing compound to get that 'as new' showroom finish.*

It's easier to spray the bonnet at this level at the same time as spraying blue coats. ▷

garage doors can stay open to give more light and the all important ventilation. Whilst drying, the gun is cleaned again using Gunwash. After 'de-nibbling' the sealed surfaces, the 2 pack paint is mixed ready to apply.

Much more to spray this time, but at least the step ladders aren't needed. Starting from the nearside back corner, David works his way along to the front taking in the top of the bulkhead and wings complete, keeping the gun on the move all the time from side to side and up and down. He retraces the air line around the front of KYJ, back along the other side and takes in the back of the vehicle. Now it's the bonnet's turn to have a new lease of life.

There's no stopping now, it's back to his starting point for the second coat, and as that's finished, it's back around again to apply the third and final coat. All the time his eyes scouring the surface as he's spraying, ensuring that each coat is even and only just thick enough to cover. The slightest stopping of the gun in one place, especially over rivits, hinges or rope hooks will only cause a run underneath.

The following morning all the masking is carefully removed revealing a very smart vehicle. The bonnet is put back and odd bits of previously removed trim are screwed back on.

Later that day, after collecting David's Range Rover from Okehampton following the fitting of the air lockers, KYJ's new paintwork is checked over. As the odd insect decided to commit suicide on the paint's wet surface a small amount of attention was needed.

These imperfections are easily put right by using a polishing mop on a rotary polisher, preferably leaving the paint to harden for two days. The affected areas have some medium/course polishing compound applied and with a little water on the mop, the polisher is kept on the move. It does no harm, in fact, to go over the whole vehicle in this manner, keeping the polisher away from both internal and external edges.

If, when respraying 'your' vehicle and the wheel centres are in reasonable condition, of course you could refurbish them by the following method. Have the five tyres removed, strip old paint with paint stripper (wear protective clothing, gloves and goggles), power wash, wire brush them and sand with 180 or 240 grit wet and dry. Then apply Etch Primer Sealer and prepare and paint as in the same manner as painting the vehicle. We managed to buy a set of five new rims ready painted at the 'right' price.

Now, I know to many of you perhaps considering respraying your Land Rover that it all sounds rather daunting all this preparation. Making a 'tent' in the garage, working out what you need in painting and sundries, hiring a compressor and gun capable of giving a steady 60psi at the gun, a D/A sander and charcoal nose and mouth mask.

If you have done most of the other work on the vehicle you will be surprised at your own results. Don't forget you could always ▷

Final polishing off by hand.

Put a sparkle back into your vehicles' bodywork, just like KYJ. The wheel rims were beyond cost effective restoration. It was cheaper to purchase a ready sprayed set of rims. This picture shows the depth of gloss achieved by using Acrylic Urethane 2 pack Enamel which is hard to get with either cellulose or synthetic paints.

practise first on a spare wing or bonnet propped up in the middle of the garage.

To help you work out what you need for a vehicle similar to KYJ, here's a list for you to follow:-

List 1

3 litres of 2 pack Acrylic Urethane Enamel — Marine Blue.
1 litre of 2 pack Acrylic Urethane Enamel — Limestone.
2 litres of 770 Hardener (790 for cold conditions).
1 litre of 2 pack high build Etch Primer Sealer.
1 litre of Thinner.
1 litre of Activator.
1 litre of 'Extra-Filler' Acrylic primer.
1 litre of 790 Express Hardener for Extra Filler.
5 litres of Gunwash.
2 litres of Bodyclean Degreaser.
3×1 litre mixing tins.

List 2

15 sheets of 400 Wet and Dry paper.
5 sheets of 1200 Wet and Dry paper.
25 D/A 80 grit opencoat.
25 D/A 180 grit opencoat.
1 litre of Plastic Padding PP50.

If you have more dents to repair than those in KYJ then you will need in proportion more of the above.

List 3

10 paint filters.
10 mixing paper cups.
5 rolls of 2″ masking tape.
5 rolls of 1″ masking tape.
3 Tack Rags.
1 small tub of medium/course polishing compound.

The above items can all be purchased at an Auto Refinisher Suppliers.

You will need the use of a compressor with an air displacement of about 8 cfm (cubic feet per minute), 50 litre air receiver and a 120 psi maximum pressure to give the required regulated gun working pressure of 60 psi. You will also need a spray gun, long enough air line and an oil/water separator regulator. The kit should include a D/A (Dual Action) sander, orbital polisher and a blow gun.

Apart from one or two panel beaters' 'dollys' (which you could no doubt hire from the same place as the compressor equipment) I would expect you would have most of the other items needed. A builders' merchant is the best place to obtain a small roll of plastic sheeting to make your spray booth.

If you take up the challenge of preparing and respraying your Land Rover, and your garage is at least six foot wider than the vehicle (you need a clear three feet each side and a little more front and back) then give it a whirl.

A week's holiday should be sufficient, the final weekend being reserved for the actual spraying, i.e. first colour Saturday morning, second colour Sunday morning. Remember it's the preparation that counts.

My grateful thanks to David Knight for his time and expertise.

Part Eight by David Bowyer

Handbrake drum and driving flange removed exposing a pair of rather worn out and oily shoes. Notice the wrongly routed speedo cable and stretched handbrake spring. ▷

The handbrake back plate removed exposing the speedo drive and bearing ▽ housing.

Essential maintenance

THE END is in sight. KYJ is nearing completion and it won't be too long before she's ready for an MOT. However, prior to taking you through the stages of carrying out a very full service during which 'everything' is checked, I thought we had better attend to the remainder of the main problem areas found whilst carrying out the report.

With the help of James Tennant at his workshop I start by removing the rear propshaft. You will remember me mentioning that this unit was fitted back to front, that there was much 'lift' of the handbrake drum and the rear diff pinion seal was leaking. In other words, a good place to start.

As I suspected, the propshaft was knackered through the splines being badly worn, a sign of poor or complete lack of maintenace. Next I removed the handbrake drum exposing much oil and filth, no wonder the brake wasn't working. The 'lift' was clearly caused by movement in the output bearing within the speedometer drive housing and in turn wearing the oil seal.

First the transfer case was drained, followed by removal of the handbrake back plate, initially the latter being hinged out of the way by the clevis pin over the top of the transfer case. Then the speedometer drive was removed. This, by the way, had it's cable wrongly routed. The housing was then removed and cleaned up with Jizer. At this point the speedometer pinion teeth and worm drive was checked for condition. No problem.

The only apparent reason for play in the bearing seemed to be caused by too many shims between the housing and the back face of the transfer case. Having cleared the shims up, initially one less (a thinner one) was replaced and the housing bolted back. With a hand on the output shaft, there was still some movement detected, so another shim was removed until there was no play at all. But one must be careful not to take out too many shims which would only serve to over tighten the shaft. It must revolve freely, with just a hint of friction.

Now, take this opportunity to replace the oil seal by simply prizing out the original, wiping the rebate in the casting clean and placing the new seal squarely to the face. Taking an appropriately large socket or short piece of pipe tap the seal into place.

It was then realised that the handbrake cylinders needed attention so it was ▷

◁ *A view of three shims that space the housing away from the transfer case.*

Removing an oil seal on the near diff pinion using a seal remover. ▷

◁ *Make sure the pinion housing is clean before fitting new oil seal.*

undone at the clevis point. With the back plate secured frimly in the vice remove the plungers of both the expander unit and the adjuster unit, but preferably one at a time! Make sure the bores are clean and that the cleaned plungers slide nicely in and out of the cylinders. If attending to the left hand adjuster first, unscrew the adjusting cone, clean and apply a little grease to the thread and cone, lightly grease the plunger and reassemble.

The right hand expander unit is similar to the other side but is, of course, operated by the handbrake. Below each plunger is a roller which is in contact with the operating rod. Strip and clean in the same manner. In our case the rubber dust excluder was split so the rod had to be undone from the clevis to replace it.

Upon reassembly of this unit refit the special spring clip. Whilst the assembly is still in the vice, attach the new pair of transmission brake shoes along with a new pair of springs if necessary, making sure the adjusting nut is backed right off.

Before refitting the assembly, refit the speedo cable drive, making sure that the cable is routed correctly above the chassis. Reassemble as per the workshop manual, reconnecting the brake linkage, not forgetting to grease the various pivot points from the lever back to the handbrake. Refit the drive flange using a new split pin to the hexagon slotted nut.

On with the brake drum and have someone jump up into the driver's seat to 'settle' the new shoes by operating the handbrake lever a few times. Then, with the handbrake off, adjust the square head of the adjuster on the backplate until the drum becomes 'tight' Slacken back one or two 'flats' until the drum turns freely. Check the operation of the lever again and finally back at the drum itself.

Now our attention turns to the rear diff as the pinion seal is obviously leaking. Have someone apply the foot brake as you remove the flange nut. Prize out the old oil seal with screwdriver or similar object.

As with fitting all new oil seals, lubricate the lips of the new seal, smear the outer periphery with jointing compound and slide back into the wiped out housing. Use a large socket or similar object to tap the seal squarely back into place.

Next I fit the new propshaft so that the splines are at the front, ie. directly behind

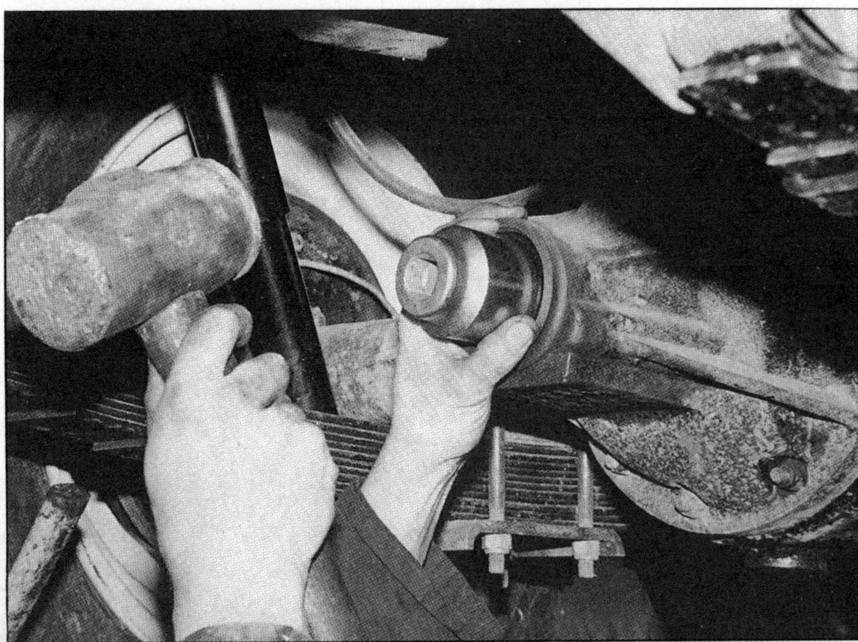

Tapping the oil seal into place. ▷ Keep checking to make sure it is square.

Old and new. The original front propshaft looking rather sorry for itself. When it last saw a grease ◁ gun is anyone's guess.

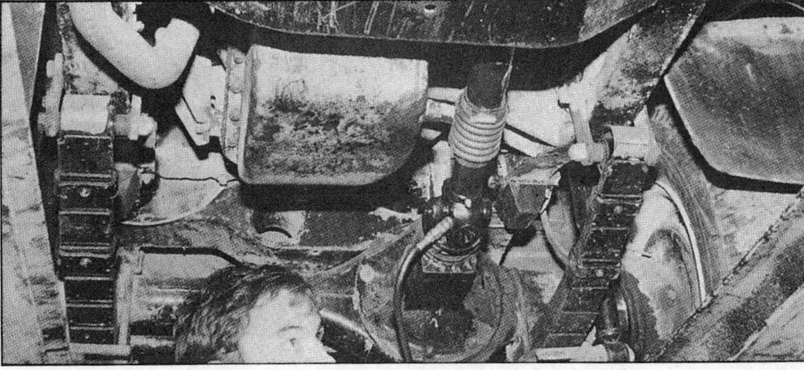

The new front propshaft gets its first greasing. ▷

the handbrake. The existing high tensile bolts are in good condition, but again as always, new Nyloc nuts are fitted.

The front differential pinion seal shows signs of weeping as well so it's off with the propshaft, off with the front drive flange and out with the seal to replace it. You will recall me mentioning that the front propshaft was well and truly knackered, so now is the time to replace it. Again, the gaited splines are to the front of the vehicle.

Before we tackle anything else we refill the tansfer case with fresh oil and grease the nipples of the four new U.J.'s and two propshaft splined joints.

Now our attention is turned to the play in the front wheel bearings. First we support the axle under the springs and with the wheel still in place, one 'feels' for the amount of play by gently moving the wheel from side to side and from top to bottom. Not only did we find quite a lot of play in both front hubs, but the nearside front sounded 'gritty' as well. So that's where we started.

After removing that wheel, the hub cap is twisted to slide off exposing the hexagon slotted nut together with split pin securing the drive flange. Following removal of the plain washer behind the nut you will find the sealing washer with its plastic face. Note which way it is fitted.

The six bolts are then removed from the drive flange which is pulled off. Slacken off the brake shoe adjuster and unscrew the two drum retaining screws. If the drum won't easily lift off the wheel studs, then insert the retaining screws into the non-countersunk threaded holes to push the drum off the hub.

As the drum came away we were confronted with an absolute mess. Oil everywhere! Obviously the bearing had worked loose, or it had never been seated properly in the beginning, allowing the oil seal to be damaged. The lock washers were then straightened securing the two hub nuts.

Usually by using a hub nut spanner the outer nut comes away easily from the locking washer allowing the inner hub nut to be almost undone by hand. Not so in this case, both nuts came out together tearing out the key of the lock washer.

The hub was then lifted off complete with bearings, outer thrust washer and oil seal. After removing the ruined brake

◁ *What a mess, no wonder the brakes didn't work.*

The right hand is holding the lock ▷ washer that sits between the two hub nuts.

◁ *A hub spanner is best for tightening the hub nuts. But don't tighten too much.*

shoes, the back plate and hub was well washed down with Jizer and dried off. I cleaned the bearings and cones and they seemed to me to be in perfect order so there was no reason to replace.

We examined the stub axle for wear, likewise the peripheral surface of the distance collar. The surface of this collar forms the running surface of the hub oil seal lip. This surface had a ridge in it and, therefore, was rendered useless. It was removed by drilling and splitting it with a cold chisel. Care must be taken so as to avoid damage to the stub axle.

Prior to fitting the inner bearing, work grease well into it first, then fit the new oil seal by placing the hub on some cloth to protect the studs. Tap the lubricated oil seal into place using the flat side of a club hammer — carefully. Place the hub into its axle, half fill with grease, and push into place the outer bearing, again well filled with grease up to its previously fitted cone.

Slide the tongued thrust washer in followed by the first nut and tighten by hand only until the hub runs freely with just a hint of friction. On with the lock tab, then the outer hub nut. Tighten this nut up against the lock tab, tight, but no need to over tighten it. Bend over the lock washer to secure one flat on each nut.

Refit the driving flange after checking for any damage to the spline using a new gasket to mate to the hub and bolt up tight using new spring washers. Fit a new felt seal, replace washer and nut. Replace the split pin and tap the hub cap back on.

Normally at this stage we would replace the brake shoes before cleaning and refitting the brake drum, but we are going to replace the shoes next month.

We finish off by carrying out much the same to the offside front. As there was far less play than its opposite number the oil seal was in much better condition. But we still stripped the hub down, repacked the bearings in the hub, fitted a new oil seal, felt seal and gasket whilst we were at it.

When carrying out this work, read and understand the appropriate sections of the workshop manual and aim to use the torque settings recommended.

Having sorted out most of the problem areas of KYJ it's on with servicing her.

Part nine by David Bowyer

△ *Removing a worn out wheel cylinder*

A thorough service

THIS MONTH we start the all important preventative maintenance programme by carrying out a full service in accordance with the vehicle's Owners Manual. There are various forms, of 'servicing,' most of which you the owner should be quite capable of carrying out with a few tools, the right lubricants and the correct replacement spares. It is important to try always to use Genuine Parts wherever possible.

"Routine maintenance" is the traditional Sunday morning check over and shouldn't take more than ten minutes or so once the vehicle is really all together. These checks are also appropriate before setting off on a long journey, a holiday, or simply before green laning.

Start from the front with the bonnet open, and engine cold.

1. Check engine oil level.
2. Check radiator level (both at the rad and expansion tank.) If a top up is necessary, have some ready made up antifreeze solution in a plastic ½ gallon container mixed at 50% strength so that when winter does come your engine will be properly protected.
3. Check brake fluid level.
4. Check clutch fluid level.
5. Check for any signs of leakage from either joint or unions in any fuel, oil or water pipes.
6. Check condition of fan belt.
7. Check that all looms and plug leads are in their rightful place and not dislodged and therefore dangling across manifold following the previous weekend green lane trip!
8. Top up the windscreen washer using an appropriate solvent. In cold weather use a stronger solution as per the instructions on the bottle.

Having satisfied yourself that all is well in this area walk around the vehicle casting your eyes underneath your pride and joy with special attention being paid to:

9. Condition of tyres, that's inner and outer sidewalls as well as the tread itself, then checking the tyre pressures. If, say during the last week, you were unfortunate enough to have had a puncture and used the spare wheel, then check the tightness of those wheel nuts again.
10. Check underneath the Land Rover just to satisfy yourself that all looks 'in order', again especially if you have recently been off roading.
11. Finally check the operation of all lights. How do you know that either a sidelight or brake light bulb hasn't blown?

Well that's not so bad is it? A brief check over regularly like this will give you peace of mind and will ensure that 'she' is always 'ready to go'.

Now let's look at "maintenance schedules". The all important recognised method of looking after and ensuring your Land Rover lasts for many years which includes a certain amount of "preventative maintenance" to see the vehicle through to it's following service.

The schedules recommended by Land Rover Ltd take the form of A and B services. From when the vehicle was new, an 'A' service would have been carried out at 6,000, 18,000, 30,000 and 42,000 mile periods. Whereas the 'B' services would have taken place at 12,000, 24,000, 36,000 and 48,000 mile times. And so on and so forth.

The trouble is even with the best of intentions these services go haywire by becoming either non-existent or fewer and farther between, which is of course a great shame from a point of reliability, safety and of course longevity.

Well, let's get the overalls on and start running down the list in order to give our project vehicle a full 'B' service, i.e. a

▷

◁ *After thoroughly cleaning the backplate and drum, a new wheel cylinder and pair of linings are fitted.*

Tapping the brake drum while finally tightening the drum screws ensures it's seating properly. ▷

12,000 mile check over. Whilst carrying out this work we will naturally attend to repairs and replacements as we go.

With the help of Darren Phare at James Tennant's workshop facility at Okehampton we start by placing KYJ up on the ramps in order to drain all the oils in one go by placing a cleaned out container under each drain point.

I shall run through our service in the order that we carried it out, but at the end of next month's article I will set out a schedule for you to follow which will enable you to carry out this work one item at a time.

Whilst draining is in progress we support the vehicle by it's axles by the ramp beams, lower the ramps a few inches in order to remove all the road wheels in order to check each brake in turn.

Start draining from the back of the vehicle with firstly the back axle, followed by the overdrive, transfer case, gearbox, engine sump, front axle, and finally the two swivel housings. You only need a small container under each of these housings, but be sure to remove the filler/level plugs to help the draining process as they have very small drain plugs.

The overdrive drain plug appeared to have been seized in it's hole for life as the only way of removing it was heating the casting around it very carefully before the plug could be removed. If it had been serviced regularly this wouldn't have been a problem!

Clean up all the plugs and fit new sealing washers ready for inserting later. When draining of all oils is finally complete, before discarding the used oil into an old 5 gallon oil drum check carefully for any bits of metal in the collection containers. You can pour the used oil through an old pair of ladies tights stretched over the top of a funnel.

Do your bit for the environment and take your old oil to your nearest recycling centre.

Better get on with the brakes now. The first job is to 'back off' the brake adjuster, so as to make removal of the drum easier. You can use the brake drum screws to push the drum off by inserting them in the threaded holes. In seconds you will determine what needs replacing. The linings will either be in good order, acceptable or worn out like all four sets on KYJ.

Also, if there are signs of brake fluid under the rubber dust caps, then the unit needs replacing like three of them on KYJ. A seal kit can be purchased for these cylinders, but as the brakes are so important, many will advise you to replace the unit.

In any case, on an old unit you will probably find either the bleed nipple is well stuck fast or the brake pipe union shears off if replacing the pipe behind.

Remove the worn out linings, noting how the springs are fitted, remove the wheel cylinder if necessary and give the back plate a good clean up with Jizer and a brush. Place an open container underneath. Clean up the brake drum too. If this is very badly scored then it will have to be replaced.

On no account attempt to blow dust out of a brake asembly. Asbestos dust will do you no good.

Fit the new wheel cylinder and at that stage check out visually the brake pipes behind attached to the axle. If in doubt you must replace.

Fit the new linings, ensuring that they are installed the right way round along with the springs. Make sure that the adjusting

The spanner ▷ mark both the drain and filler/level plugs on the front swivel housings.

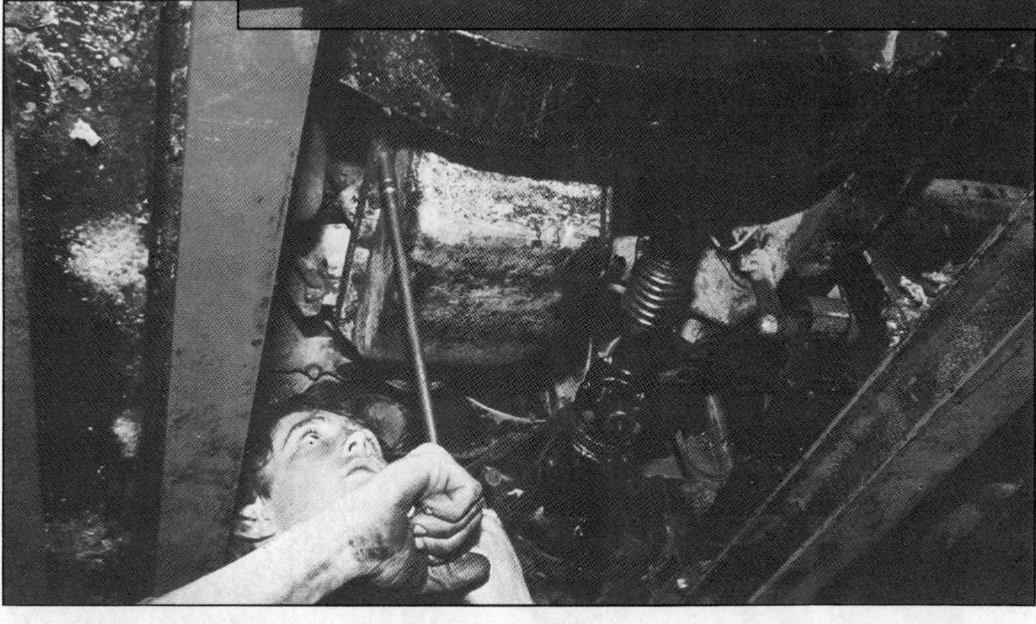

Tightening the sump bolts. Also check the transfer case while you're at it. ◁

nut is backed right off before placing the cleaned drum back over the studs. The countersunk holes must line up over the threaded hose.

Tighten the screws with a large well-fitting screwdriver and finish off by tapping the drum as you finally tighten the screws. Incidentally, if the screw heads are in poor shape buy a new set.

Apply just a spot of Coppergrease to the wheel studs in preparation for refitting the wheels later.

When all four brakes have been attended to, check over thoroughly the remainder of the brake system, starting with the flexible pipes and working your way along the chassis up to the reservoir. Replace items as required.

Have someone help you now to set up and bleed the system.

It is recommened that brake linings, hose and pipes should be examined at intervals no greater than those laid down in the maintenance schedules of the handbook. Brake fluid should be changed completely every 18 months or 18,000 miles whichever is the sooner.

All fluid seals in the hydraulic system and all flexible hoses should be renewed every three years or 36,000 miles whichever is the sooner. At the same time the working surfaces of the piston and the bores of the master cylinders, wheel cylinders, and other slave cylinders should be examined and new parts fitted where necessary.

Having got the brakes sorted out it's time to replenish all oils. Starting with the back of the vehicle, the drain plug is inserted into the axle casing and the filler/level plug is unscrewed. And in goes about three pints of nice clean 90 EP gear oil followed by the plug. Then it's the turn of the overdrive, transfer case, gearbox, front diff and the two front swivel housings.

Next the engine oil must be replaced, but only after we unscrewed the oil filter casing. A clean way of removing this unit without getting oil down inside your sleeves is to cut away the thin side of a plastic 5 litre oil container and hold directly under the unit after initially loosening the centre bolt. And you catch the lot, in the pot!

Clean out the unit after discarding the filter element in Jizer, but be careful not to loose the spring and special washer. Insert new element, and replace the unit making sure it sits up squarely into it's housing against it's seal.

Now's a good time to check the tightness of all the sump securing bolts. The 'dry' engine takes just over 12 pints of 15W/50 engine oil. We checked the level later after the engine was run a while.

Finally whilst changing oils, the oil bath air cleaner is stripped, emptied, cleaned in Jizer and refilled with engine oil, ready for putting back in the vehicle. In all we used 14 pints of engine oil and 17 pints of gear oil. That's nearly four gallons of oil we've replaced, sure is a lot of oil.

As Darren and I are working generally both around and in the engine compartment it's a good time to undo and clean out the fuel sediment bowl which is located on the right hand side of the engine behind the petrol pump.

Care must be taken when slackening the thumb screw in order to swing the retainer to one side that, (a) you don't get an eye full of petrol and (b) you don't drop the glass bowl. Clean the filter gauge in petrol and check the condition of the sealing washer. After replacing the gauze and refitting the bowl, prime the pump beside by operating the lever. Ensure there are no leaks.

Next job is to replace the contact points in the distributor, setting the gap to 0.33 to 0.40mm (0.014 to 0.016 in) with the

▷

◁ *Adjusting the gap of the contact points in the distributor. It's a good idea to replace the condenser every other major 'B' service.*

The tappet's turn for adjustment. However if the gap is right, leave alone and check the next. ▷

feeler gauge a 'sliding fit' between the contacts.

Before replacing the rotor arm, lightly smear the cam with grease, but do not oil the cam wiping pad. Add a few drops of oil to the felt pad in the top of the cam spindle, also through the gap in the base plate to lubricate the advance mechanism.

Now add just a drop of oil to the moving plate bearing groove. Carefully clean the rotor cam with fine emery cloth and refit by twisting until it pushes fully home. Wipe out the inside of the distributor cap and replace.

Finally check that all the high tension leads are clean, well fitted, clear of one another and that none are resting on any part of the engine. The above is applicable to the Lucas unit, but the Ducellier is similar. Follow the handbook.

Remove at this stage the rocker cover to expose the tappets. Now remove the sparking plugs, but make sure that no mud or dirt surrounding the plug can fall in as it is taken out.

Use the tyre gauge or airline to clear out this area first. If the plugs look in very new condition, they may be cleaned and reset. If you have no idea and they look worn, then replace them with the correct type, setting gaps to 0.75 to 0.80mm (0.029 to 0.032in).

To finish the day off, before inserting the spark plugs Darren adjusts the tappets, the rocker cover being removed first before taking the sparking plugs out to minimise the possibility of dislodging more dirt that might fall into the cylinders. To adjust the tappets rotate the engine in it's normal direction with the starting handle until the valve receiving attention is fully open, and then rotate the engine one complete turn to bring the tappet onto the back of the cam.

Now check the tappet clearance with the appropriate feeler gauge. If adjustment is required, slacken the locknut with a ring spanner, and rotate the tappet adjusting screw until the clearance is correct. When you have the feelers a 'sliding fit,' re-tighten the locknut taking care that in so doing, this doesn't upset the clearance.

Do each valve in turn using the ring spanner as a marker for the next one to do. Now fit the sparking plugs, do not over tighten.

Clean up the rocker cover in Jizer together with it's attached breather. When clean and dry secure a new gasket to it's underside with some impact adhesive. Replace the rocker cover using a smear of Hylomar on it's mating surface with the engine.

Well that's a good day's work for the two of us, we run the engine for a while to satisfy ourselves that all is in order. Remember to follow every applicable section in the owners manual when carrying out the work. The only specialist piece of equipment we needed was in fact the oxy-acetylene torch to help remove the overdrive drain plug, I think we were unlucky.

● Next month we shall complete this major service.

Δ *Oil every joint along the length of the accelerator linkage*

◁ *No wonder the operation of the clutch packed up. A badly siezed slave cylinder*

Service schedule

I THINK we are winning. This month we complete the major service and at the same time ensure that the Rover is ready to have her MOT. Back again at James Tennant's workshop, Darren Phare and myself continue with the work.

However, the first problem to confront us is that the clutch fails to work. On investigation the slave cylinder is found to be totally knackered, as it is siezed solid. During the last few months the clutch operation has, in fact, been deteriorating. Fortunately replacing this unit is not a difficult job, but when bleeding the hydraulic system we think that soon the master cylinder seals may need replacing.

Having got that sorted out perhaps we had better get on with the service.

Following the Service Schedule at the end of this chapter, we cross off all the items appropriate for our 4-cylinder petrol vehicle as the work is completed.

First we check the level of the EP90 oil in the steering box. Low is not the word. It was so low that we automatically changed it anyway.

This was followed by checking the condition and security of the steering box. This was done by turning the steering wheel from side to side about a quarter of a turn whilst one 'feels' for any movement between itself and it's adjacent bracket and chassis mounting point.

We check too all the steering ball joints commonly known as 'track rod ends' for both condition of the rubber boots which keeps the original grease in and mud and water out, and for wear.

Any wear in the joint is detected whilst the joint is moved vigorously up and down. Have someone move the steering wheel from side to side too whilst your hand covers each joint in turn.

Don't forget the steering connecting the steering box drop arm to the top of the relay. I can only think that KYJ must have had all her ball joints replaced before her last MOT nearly two years ago as not one needed changing. Neither was there any backlash in the system.

Although we check the battery next, greasing terminals, checking level and specific gravity of the electrolyte we know the battery is on it's way out, as invariably it has to be charged once a month to move it.

Next it's the turn of the cooling and heater system for checking. Every single hose is carefully looked at for condition and all jubilee clips are checked for tightness. The anti-freeze strength is also checked, especially as we are now into winter.

The windscreen washer bottle is drained, cleaned out and refilled with the appropriate solution of additive. All tubes are checked for condition. I go to check the operation of the windscreen washers. Typi-

▷

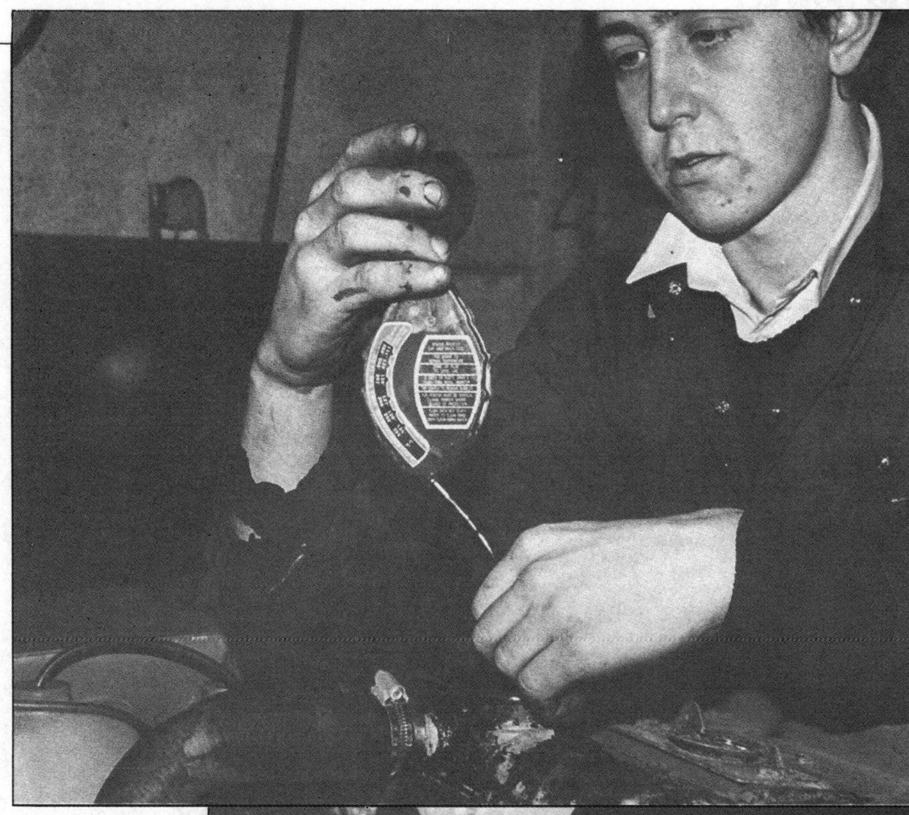

Darren Phare checks the strength of the radiator coolant

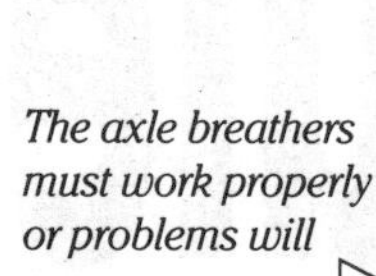

The axle breathers must work properly or problems will occur

cal, they don't work. The pump is not operating next to the reservoir. Earth is checked – OK. Power to the unit – OK. Out with the pump, into the bin. Fit new pump. All is fine … adjust spray to hit just under the top of each screen.

Before checking the fan belt we know that the alternator bearing must be totally shot as it sounded horrible. So off it comes. You could feel the grinding of the bearing by turning the pulley by hand. No way round it. We had to fit one new alternator – service exchange, of course, – using the original pulley and fan. At least we saved on the fitting of a new fan belt as that was in good condition. Don't over tighten the belts, as that is the usual cause of ruining alternator bearings.

The ignition timing was checked next using a strobe light in accordance with the manual and needed no alteration. This is easy to do following the manual.

As regards the crankcase breather system there are several types fitted on Series III vehicles. Our model has it's breather valve fitted next to the carburettor. The cover was removed exposing a horrible mess inside. It was cleaned out, diaphragm checked and reassembled. The engine breather fitted to the top of the rocker cover was cleaned when we removed it to check the tappets.

Having checked just about everything in the engine compartment we check underneath. We have already checked all the steering system other than the steering relay. I removed the grille and the plate above the relay in order to take out **only two** of the small bolts in the top of the unit in order to fill with oil.

Unscrew just the front and back ones. Leave the other two well alone. You fill the unit through the front exposed hole allowing air to escape out of the back hole. Keep filling with the oil can until oil comes out of the back hole, then replace the screws.

Next on the agenda is checking the operation of the handbrake, adjusting and lubricating the unit. Like the rest of the braking system the handbrake is very important.

Whilst underneath, remove and check both the front and rear axle case breathers. You should be able to hear the rattle of the ball inside when shaken. They cannot be stripped. You can try soaking them overnight to loosen the stuck ball bearing. But, if that doesn't work, throw them away and replace.

If you are an off-roader, replace them with the later remote type as fitted to Ninety/One Ten. With the later type there's nothing to go wrong – unless they work loose and get ripped off.

We now carry out a final check inside the vehicle. The interior lights, warning indicators in the dashboard, the horn, wiper operation, and heater controls are all checked.

Seats and seat belts are next. Make sure the seat bases and backs are located prop-

Feeling for wear on the steering ball joint ▷

The crankcase valve before cleaning ▽

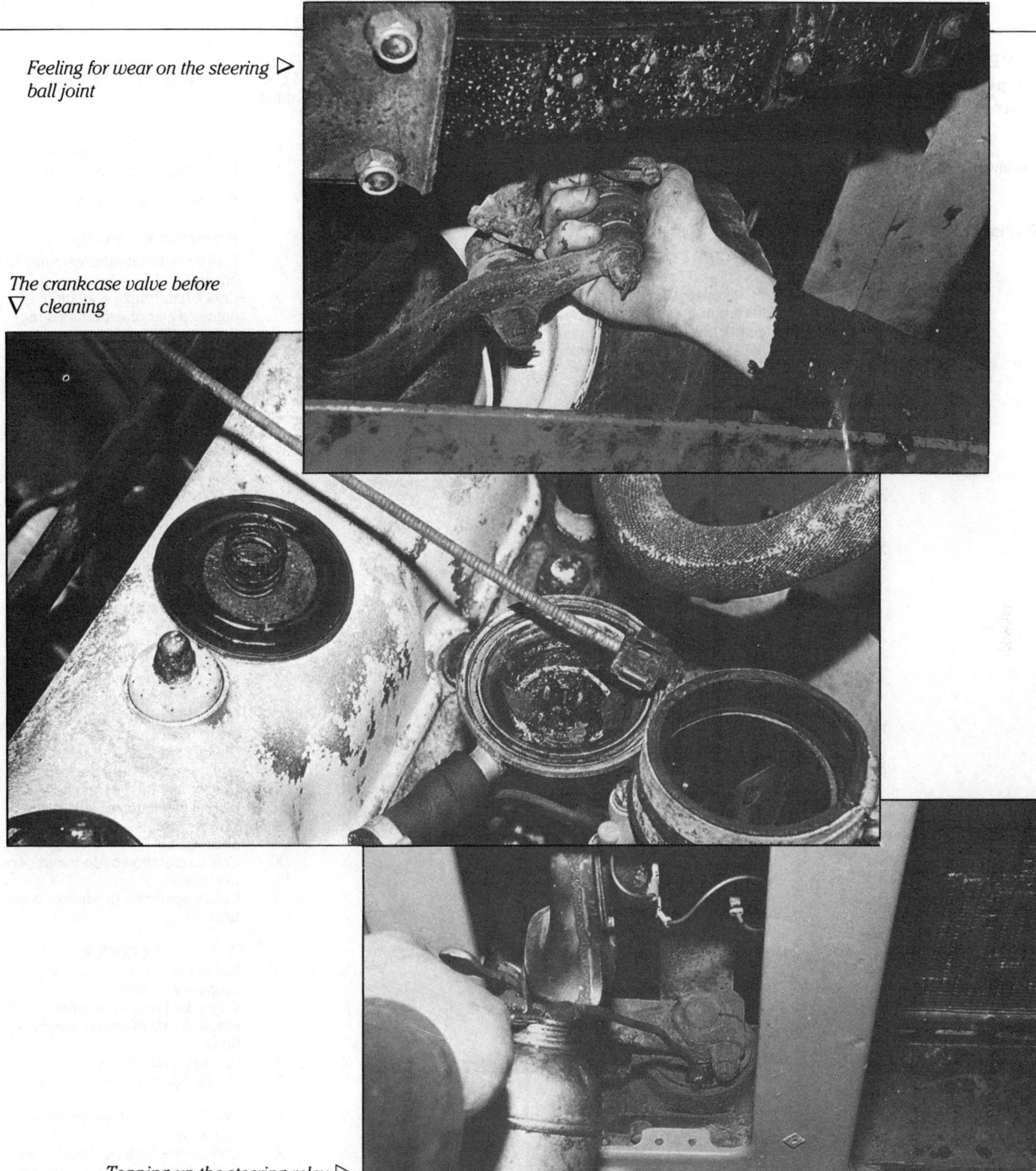

Topping up the steering relay ▷

erly, including those in the back if they are fitted. Of extreme importance is the condition and security of the seat belts along with their mountings, buckles and inertia reel mechanism if fitted. The slightest fraying of a belt will be a fail item on an MOT test.

Mirrors, both interior and exterior, are they adjusted right? And fitted securely? They must also be in good condition and free of cracks and crazing.

Clean and re-oil all the door locks and bonnet catch and whilst at it apply a little oil to the door hinges. Ensure all window catches work and glass runners are clean and rot free.

We finish off around the exterior of KYJ. The condition of the tyres and pressures are checked. The tightness of the wheel nuts. Don't forget the spare.

The headlight beam setting alignment will need to be checked, especially after changing a sealed beam unit. This can be done at night facing a closed garage door or wall following the manual's instructions. Or simply ask your friendly MOT station to do it for you, if required. Make sure that every exterior lamp functions properly and that the lenses are in good order. Check too the windscreen wiper blades are in good condition.

From time to time the front wheel alignment ought to be checked. This is best done when the vehicle is visiting a tyre depot for tyre changing and balancing. These people are equipped to do the job properly.

Finally, following a weekend's work on your pride and joy, go for a road test specifically to check that all you have done, works properly.

Remember the manuals which cover your vehicle are there to help you as everything is covered. Most servicing work can be carried out with a simple range of tools. Perhaps you are short of a particular item. For instance a strobe light for setting/checking the ignition timing. You have only got to buy one once. Tools are a lifetime investment.

We still have a few items to finish off on KYJ. Chassis to finish painting, wayoyling, undersealing, rear seats to fit, windscreen glasses to change, rear side windows to install.

Next page: Servicing schedules

COVERING all Series III models, both 4 and 6 cylinder petrol and 4 cylinder diesel – home and export models.

Weekly	Monthly	Every 6,000 miles	Every 12,000 miles	Operation *Diesel operation in italics*
Routine Checks		A	B	
				ENGINE COMPARTMENT
	X	X	X	Check for oil leaks
		X	X	Check/top-up steering box
		X	X	Check condition and security of steering box
			X	Check/adjust steering backlash
X	X	X	X	Check/top-up clutch fluid reservoir
X	X	X	X	Check/top-up brake fluid reservoir
			X	Clean fuel pump sediment bowl (4 cyl)
			X	Renew fuel filter element (6 cyl)
		X	X	Renew engine flame trap
		X	X	Lubricate accelerator linkage and check operation
		X	X	Top-up carburettor piston damper – if that type of unit is fitted
			X	*Check injectors for burst pressure and test for spray*
			X	*Check condition of heater plug wiring for fraying, chafing and deterioration*
			X	Clean air cleaner filter and renew oil
			X	Check/adjust distributor points
		X	X	Renew distributor points
			X	Lubricate distributor
		X		Clean/adjust spark plugs
			X	Renew spark plugs
			X	Clean engine breather filter
	X	X	X	Check/top-up battery electrolyte
		X	X	Clean and grease battery connections
X	X	X	X	Check/top-up cooling system
		X	X	Check all cooling/heater system hoses for security and condition
X	X	X	X	Check/top-up windscreen washer reservoir
	X	X	X	Check driving belts, adjust or renew
			X	Check/adjust valve clearances
		X	X	Check/adjust ignition timing and distributor using electronic equipment
X	X			Check/top-up engine oil
			X	*Renew fuel filter element (diesel models)*
	every 36,000 miles			Renew brake servo air filter (where fitted)
		X		Check crankshaft breathing system for leaks, hoses for security and condition
			X	Clean and test crankcase breather valve
			X	Check air injection system/pipes for security and condition if applicable
			X	Check/adjust air pump drive belt if applicable
				UNDERBODY
	X	X	X	Check for oil leaks
		X	X	Check condition and security of steering relay unit, joints and gaiters
		X	X	Check/top-up steering relay
		X	X	Check/top-up front axle oil
	every 24,000 miles			Renew front axle oil
		X	X	Check/top-up swivel pin housings oil
		X	X	Renew engine oil
		X	X	Renew engine oil filter
X	X	X	X	Drain flywheel housing if drain plug fitted for wading
			X	*Clean fuel sediment (diesel models)*
	every 48,000 miles			Clean fuel pump filter (6 cyl models)

Weekly	Monthly	Every 6,000 miles	Every 12,000 miles	Operation *Diesel operation in italics*
Routine Checks		A	B	
		X	X	Check/top-up main gearbox oil
		X	X	Check/top-up transfer box oil
	every 24,000 miles			Renew main gearbox oil
	every 24,000 miles			Renew transfer box oil
		X	X	Lubricate handbrake mechanical linkage
		X	X	Check handbrake operation: adjust to manufacturer's instructions
		X	X	Lubricate propeller shafts
	every 24,000 miles			Lubricate propeller shaft sealed sliding portion
		X	X	Check/top-up rear axle oil
	every 24,000 miles			Renew rear axle oil
	X	X	X	Check exhaust system for leaks and security
			X	Check visually fuel pipes for chafing, leaks and corrosion
		X	X	Check visually brake/clutch hydraulic pipes and unions for chafing, leaks and corrosion
			X	Clean front and rear axle case breathers
				PASSENGER COMPARTMENT
	X	X	X	Check function of original equipment, i.e. interior lamps, horns, heater controls, wiper, and warning indicators
		X	X	Check condition and security of seats, seat belts and buckles
		X	X	Check operation of seat belt inertia reel mechanism (where fitted)
		X	X	Check rear view mirror for cracks and crazing
		X	X	Check operation of door and bonnet locks
		X	X	Check operation of window controls
				EXTERIOR
		X	X	Inspect brake linings for wear, drums for condition
		X	X	Check foot brake operation: adjust to manufacturer's instructions
		X	X	Change road wheels
	X	X	X	Check tightness of road wheel nuts
	X	X	X	Check and adjust tyre pressures incl. spare
	X	X	X	Check tyres for tread depth, cuts in tyre fabric exposure of ply or cord structure
		X	X	Check/adjust headlight alignment
X	X	X	X	Check all exterior lights
		X	X	Check, if necessary renew wiper blades
		X	X	Check/adjust front wheel alignment
				ROAD TEST
		X	X	Road test and check function of all instrumentation
				PREVENTATIVE MAINTENANCE
	every 18,000 miles			Renew hydraulic brake fluid
	every 36,000 miles			Renew rubber seals in brake system

Note: If your vehicle covers less than 12,000 miles a year then carry out the 'A' Service every 6 months and the 'B' Service every 12 months.

Why not photocopy this schedule so you can cross off the items as you complete each task?

Part eleven by David Bowyer

◁ *There's no short cut to replacing swivel housing seals. Removal of the unit is the only way. The new seal is the top one.*

Just look at the wear on the splines in the right hand old drive flange ▷

The backbone

WITH THE service now completed it's time to finish off one or two other important jobs prior to painting the chassis.

One of the jobs I've been meaning to do for a while is to change the front swivel housing seals. It is very important that these large seals do not allow oil to leak out because, should the housing run dry, the steering will tighten through lack of lubrication to say nothing of the reduced life of the universal joint contained within the housing.

Remember too, that poor seals will allow water and mud to penetrate and cause further problems.

Both sides needed new seals. With the vehicle well supported after removing the front wheels, the appropriate track rod ends were removed with the ball joint extractor. The flexible brake pipes were then disconnected from the new wheel cylinders after pinching them first, to contain brake fluid in the system.

All the bolts securing the inboard oil seal covers were extremely stubborn and needed heat from a torch to facilitate removal. Note the position of the steering stop and brake hose brackets in this area.

Next the bolts and nuts securing the inner flange of the swivel housing assembly to the axle flanges need undoing. These were jolly stubborn, too. Allow plenty of time here to change these seals and what's that saying - patience is a virtue.

With the assembly withdrawn from the axle, remove and discard the flange gasket followed by prizing out the oil seal itself. Wipe clean both the housing and the cover and remove all traces of dirt and grit from the polished housing surface.

Apply Blue Hylomar to the housing to ensure oil cannot escape behind the seal. Liberally coat surface of the seal with EP90 and push squarely into place and secure with the cover.

If any difficulty is found in inserting the six bolts, run a tap through to clean the threads in the housing.

Fit the housings back to the threads using new gaskets and new nuts, not forgetting to refit the steering stop bracket. Adjust the lock stops to suit the tyres fitted and reconnect the track rod ends using new split pins. Check the lock stops again after the track rod is connected.

I hasten to add, only tackle one swivel housing at a time as twenty four stubborn bolts in one go is likely to try your patience. Check the oil levels before you forget.

Another job I've been meaning to do is change both front drive flanges, as much wear in the splines had taken place.

I had a spare set of flanges from when fitting some freewheel hubs onto one of my own Series IIIs some years ago. These were used for replacement along with new gaskets, felt seals, split pins and a matching pair of hub caps.

As Darren and I had lost a good half day carrrying out these operations, it was time to change the mudshields under the front wings. These thin metal panels take a real hammering from mud and water being thrown up constantly against them from the front wheels.

They are not likely to last that number of years in any case as, through design, they trap water and filth behind them which only seems to accelerate their corrosion.

Again, much patience is needed to remove the existing bolts and nuts. In the end I gave up with traditional methods and attacked the bolts with the grinderette working from under the wing.

Even with the overall's collar buttoned up, wearing a hat, goggles and gloves, it's a horrible job. It's like having your nose right

▷

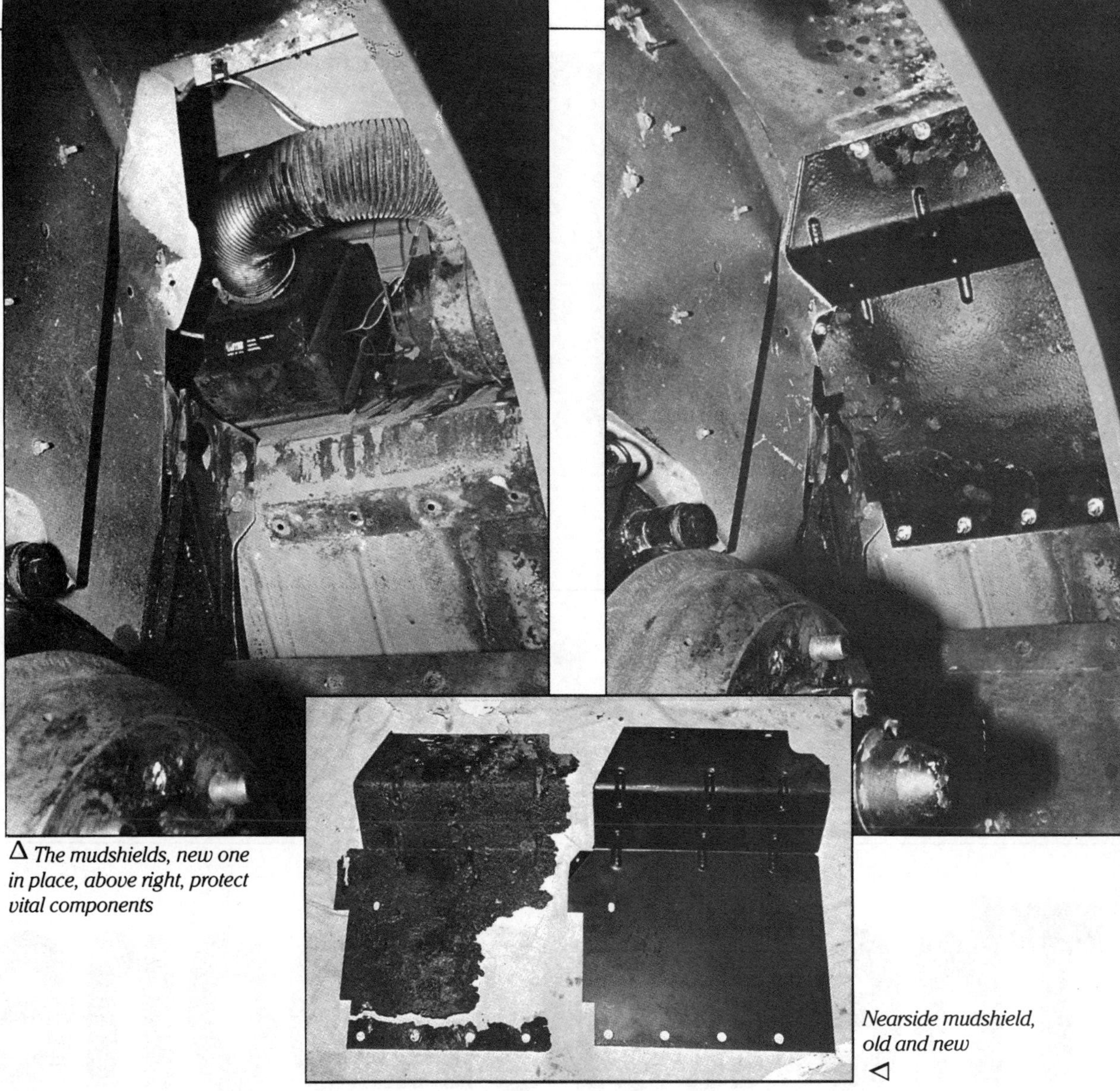

Δ *The mudshields, new one in place, above right, protect vital components*

Nearside mudshield, old and new ◁

up in front of a 'catherine wheel', with your head inside a tin box and totally deafening you. Thanks Darren for doing the other side.

The replacement panels were again supplied by PWB Replacement Motor PartsLtd from Warwick and they fitted perfectly when held up in place.

Although these new mudshields are supplied painted black, it's a jolly good idea to apply a coat of underseal to them first an hour or two before fitting. We coated them each both sides.

With fresh plated nuts, bolts and washers they were soon secured into position. That left the steering box mudshield to refit being tucked up under the steering box. The oil in the general vicinity saved this part from corrosion. We simply cleared up the original, and undersealed it before refitting.

And so onto the chassis, the backbone of the vehicle. Having spent so much time and effort on KYJ, it is so necessary to protect the chassis from further corrosion.

I would be failing in my duty to forgo this vital final major part of the refurbishment. To simply take her out onto the road now, or worse still, to go green laning without further thought to carrying out some sort of preventative maintenance to ensure longevity of the vehicle would be ludicrous.

If one wants to keep one's 'pride and joy' for a good few years, then believe me this next part of our refurbishment is the most important of all. We have already paid the cost of having to renew the back of the chassis, all the outriggers bar one, and the need to plate and repair the main chassis rails each side under the rear body.

The first job whilst the vehicle's dry underneath is to finish scraping the surface rust and filth off. Wearing goggles, start at one corner, methodically cleaning the surface back using a four or five row wire brush and a one inch wide paint scraper or old knife. Scrape and wire brush every square inch of the chassis.

The job was made easier for me as, apart from the initial extensive cleaning with a power washer some nine months ago, I've also taken every opportunity whilst working under the vehicle to clean up sections from time to time.

For instance, the chassis was cleaned and painted along most of the outsides during and after the replacing of all the outriggers.

There are some parts of the chassis where you simply cannot get a wire brush to, such as along the top, under the floor. But in most cases you can get the scraper in and can wrap some rough sandpaper around it which works quite well.

Having satisfied yourself that you've done the best job you can, the next thing to do is to prepare the chassis for 'inside' treatment as well. I'm not going to suggest that we are to spray paint inside the sections. The only good method of treating the inside is using Waxoyl later after the paint is dry.

So, looking ahead to allow for Waxoyling, some extra holes are needed to poke the lance through. This brings me to a topic of discussion close to my heart as an off-roader.

Whenever you take your 4x4 through deep water and mud you are always going to partly fill the chassis and outrigger sections with the muck. Inevitably this is what causes the start of the rot in the first place.

On the basis that you can't stop the muck getting in, then give some consideration to ensuring it gets out again pretty promptly. Simply enlarge the various holes already along the underside of the chassis, rear cross-member, centre cross-members and

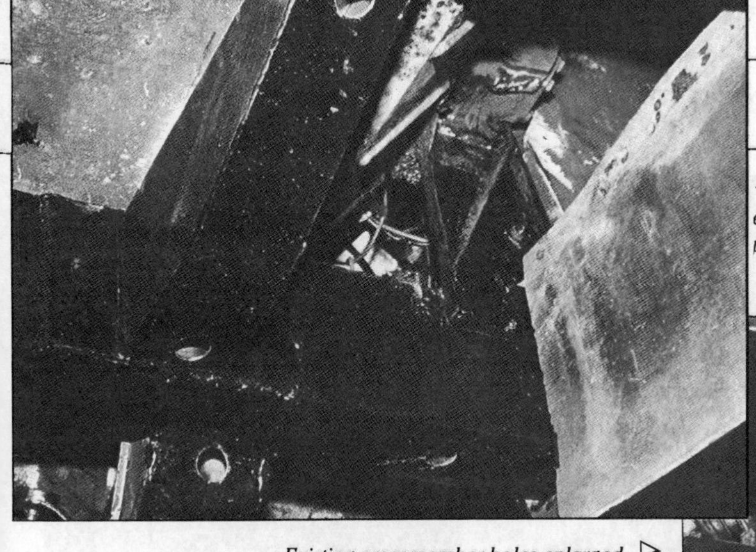

◁ *This picture4 shjpws four of the either new or enlarged holes used as drain and Waxoyl injection points*

Existing crossmember holes enlarged. ▷

Hopefully saved front dumbiron after drilling this drainage ▽ *hole*

The underside starting to look new again with its fresh coat of paint ▷

box section outriggers. Then drill some more holes at all the lowest points and in between at no more than eighteen inch intervals.

For the new holes, use a pilot drill first and enlarge them by using a stepped or cone cutter. This is the type of cutter you use when drilling large holes to fit aerials in wings. Ideally the holes want to be about ⅞" diameter. When carrying out this work wear goggles and gloves, the gauntlet type if you can lay your hands on to a pair. The strings of metal that come off these cutters are very hot.

All the closed box sections need at least two holes drilled so as to apply the Waxoyl from both ends. Finish off these large holes with a round file.

One place you definitely need to drain is in between the two front bumper bolt nuts in the spring hanger. A ½" hole will have to suffice here though.

Another place is at the very back of the chassis rails in the rear cross-member section. It's the rust that forms through water and muck being trapped here in this area between the chassis rails and rear cross-member that causes such problems.

This is followed by the absolute necessity to enlarge or drill more holes in the underside of the rear cross-member itself.

Also drill a large hole in front of the rear bump stops. This is a good place to insert the Waxoyl later as it can flow down each side of the arch in the chassis.

You can now attack the chassis inside and out with a blow gun running off the compressor, wearing the goggles, of course. This will remove the dust and debris, especially from the crevices.

Now, if we are going to spray the chassis why not take this opportunity of spraying the axles complete with springs and front track rods etc. Wire brush the axles, the springs, brake drums and backplates, and all the associated items. A cloth moistened in Gunwash will help remove oil around the lower part of the diffs and swivel housings. Finish off with the blow gun.

Get some inch-wide masking tape and mask the threaded area of the wheel studs, the brake bleed nipples on the wheel cylinders, the rubbers of the track rod ends, flexible brake hoses, bump stops and what have you.

Mask also the silencer, tail pipe and exhaust brackets. I did not try to mask the rest of the exhaust system as it was easier to clean the over-spray off with Gunwash after completing the painting.

For painting I used an ordinary spray gun which I part filled with smooth black Hammerite mixed two parts of paint to one part Hammerite thinners.

Adorned with a face mask I started at one point and worked my way right around the whole chassis applying a first 'thin' coat. Then I took in the axles and springs keeping the gun on the move all the time.

As I finished the second axle it was back to the starting point of the chassis, and so I kept going, applying four coats in all to every bit of 'bare' metal I could find. This included body stiffening straps and front mudflap brackets.

Four litres of smooth black Hammerite and two and a half litres of thinner were used in all. Half a litre of Gunwash was used to clean the gun.

After removing all the masking tape and cleaning the exhaust system and swivel housing with Gunwash it was time to call it a day. What I call a satisfying day.

Next job is to apply Waxoyl to both inside and outside the chassis and to underseal the wheel arches and floor pan - another day.

Part Twelve by David Bowyer

Δ *Puttying front windscreen rebates after cleaning out the old sealant*

Finishing touches

BEFORE CARRYING on with Waxoyling the chassis and undersealing the floorpan and wheel arches, Darren and I at James Tennant's workshop carry out a few more essential items.

Following a fifteen mile road test with James driving on trade plates, a few more items came to light. When one takes a vehicle out on test, one must be very conscious that something might go wrong. That's not to say that one mustn't believe in one's own capability in one's own work, but you must be aware of problems occurring. After all, in our case KYJ hasn't been driven much more than twenty miles in the last two years.

First we noticed a squeak coming from the direction of the speedo, a sort of dry squeak. Then as it started raining, the wiper motor becoming squeaky too.

Other than that, everything sounded just fine, perhaps a little too much whine from the overdrive unit, but one can live with that.

However, within a mile of returning to the workshop. three rather important things came to light. We could sense a 'clonk' in the steering, the sort of feeling you have when a track rod end is very badly worn.

Then the clutch didn't feel quite right according to James. He guessed it was time to change the master cylinder seals. We had reckoned to do that job in any case.

But the biggest shock was, as we were driving back into the workshop, fortunately doing only about 10 mph, James exclaimed (I won't repeat exactly what he said) "The brakes are failing" Well, would you believe it. By the time we had KYJ onto the ramp and depressed the brake pedal a few more times, the pedal went right down to the floor with no hint of any resistance.

After our mid-morning coffee, thanks Melanie, whilst James carries on working sorting out a client's Range Rover, Darren and I carry on sorting out KYJ. Will we ever finish I think! In the order of importance we identify the reasons that caused the faults.

The brakes had failed simply because the perishing little rubber pipe at the bottom of the fluid reservoir was perished! During the last three or four months for various reasons we have had need to bleed the brakes several times, so neither of us had given any thought to the fact that the fluid was down a bit each time before topping up the reservoir.

And, when I was cleaning back the chassis ready for painting, I noticed oil or fluid under the steering box. I thought it was a leak from the steering box and after wiping the chassis clean with thinners I didn't give it a second thought. Well, there's another lesson learnt. Always investigate the source of any leaks.

We replaced the perishing pipe and bled the system for hopefully the last time.

The clutch problem as James thought was the master cylinder which was in need of an overhaul. This was done by removing the unit, cleaning thoroughly whilst dismantling on the bench inspecting for wear, there was none, replacing the seals and reassembling. Darren refitted the unit and more bleeding was carried out.

With brakes and clutch soon sorted out what was the 'clonk' in the steering? Up into the drivers seat I go to turn the steering wheel from side to side whilst Darren 'feels', for movement at the many track rod

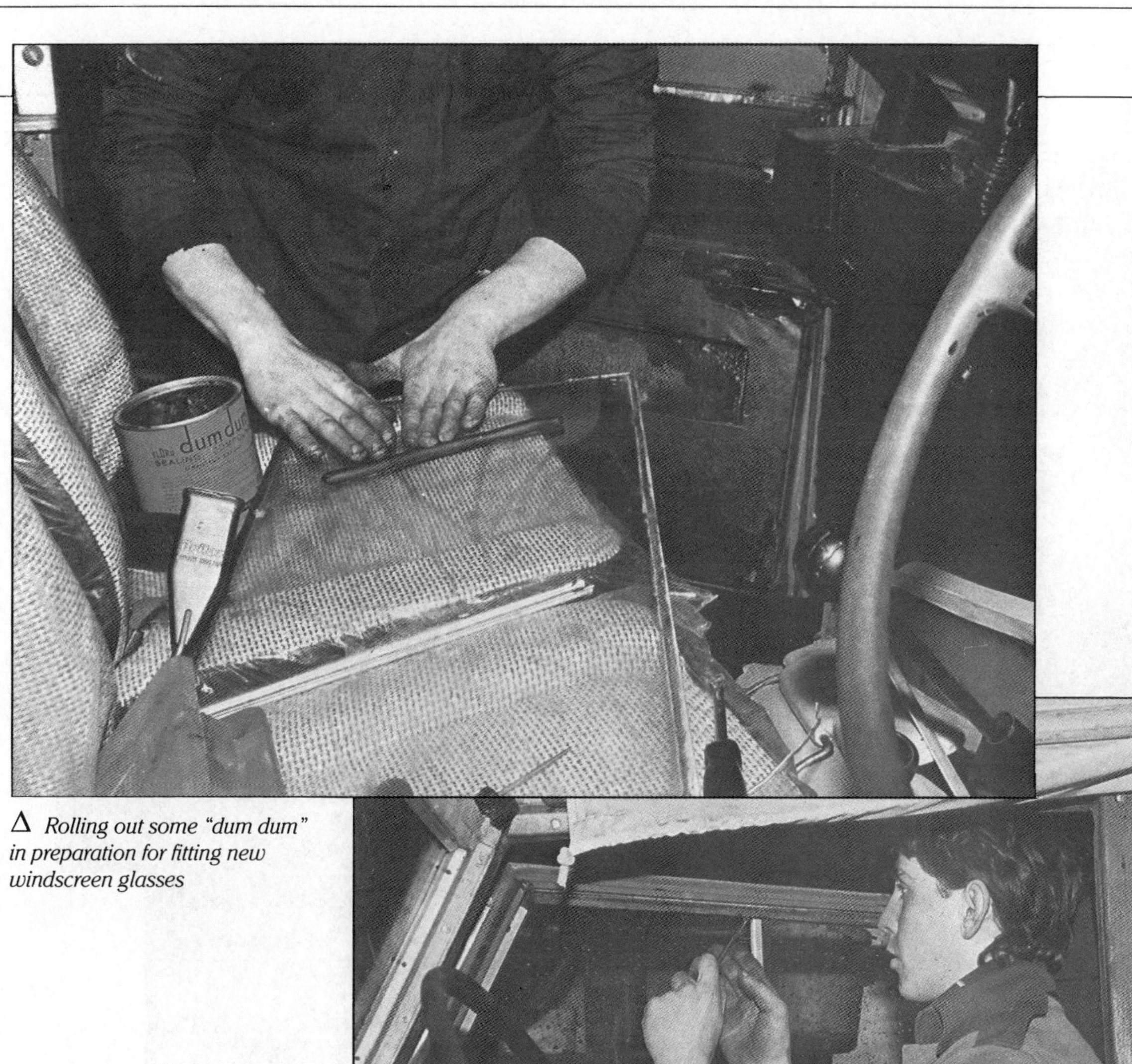

Δ *Rolling out some "dum dum" in preparation for fitting new windscreen glasses*

Removing worn out sliding window channels ▷

ends. A face appears beside the Land Rover. "It's all OK underneath. I'll take off the radiator grille to check the ball joints above the relay."

A minute later as I start turning that steering wheel again, "Found it. It's the joint above the relay, it's knackered. Keep turning. I'll climb up on the ramp and check the steering box drop arm ball joint. No that's OK".

Well, we thoroughly checked all those joints before and we remarked then how good they all seemed. We removed the longitudinal steering tube ball joint by unbolting and lifting the upper relay lever to draw it forward through the aperture.

Having removed the worn out ball joint, it was amazing to find out the huge amount of wear that was in it. We came to the conclusion that internal rust had taken up the wear and that our first major drive around the lanes had cleaned out the rust allowing it to go sloppy.

A new joint was fitted and all was reassembled with much time being spent on ensuring the steering was set right in accordance with the book of words.

The wiper motor gearbox just required some grease as it was running dry. Finally, the speedo head squeak was cured by undoing the drive from the back, putting a little grease around the spindle drive and placing a few drops of engine oil down the drive cable.

The day is moving on now and it's time to replace the front windscreen glasses as they are both badly scored by worn out wiper blades. After removing the inside trim above the windscreen together with the sun visors and wiper arms and blades, we were ready to remove all those tiny screws securing the glass retaining strips. Aren't there a lot!

With a pair of hands both from inside and outside, the glass was carefully eased into the vehicle. After much scraping of old sealant from both the galvanised windscreen rebates and retaining strips we were ready to fit the new glasses.

Lengths of dum dum were rolled out on one of the old screens and squeezed into place around each screen rebate in turn followed by the new glass being pressed in firmly. The retaining strips were screwed back into place. When both glasses were in, the surplus of dum dum was neatly removed from the front edges of the glasses using a putty knife. A little meths was ideal to clean the new glasses up. Wow, what a difference, it's nice to see out!

Incidentally, I always wondered why the interior light never worked even after checking the bulb. Now I know why, for when I unscrewed the centre retaining strip, the supply wire behind was broken in two, severed by one of the screws.

Next job on the agenda, and last to finish off the day, was to replace all the sliding window channels of both side doors. First the fabric was scraped out of the channels with an old screwdriver, then the screws were unscrewed with difficulty so some were driven out sideways with the blunt screwdriver. Eventually the top channels came free and after removing the rubber stops, the sliding glass was inclined inwards complete with top channel. The remaining bits of channel were removed in much the same way being careful not to damage the shim pieces.

Top, bottom and side channels were cut from lengths supplied by our now good friends in the trade, PWB Replacement Motor Parts Ltd of Warwick. The bottom

▷

Δ *With the painting and waxoyling complete, next job is undersealing, using a proper gun that the cannister screws into* ▷

channels need slots drilling and filing out to take the window lock mechanism.

I took this opportunity to thoroughly clean both the sliding and fixed window glasses before reinstalling the sliding units. By the way, do make sure you have plenty of those small countersunk screws handy when carrying out this job won't you, because you will be lucky to use many of the old ones.

With both sliding windows fitted with the new channels it was time to call it a day.

Next morning as it was nice outside we decide to fit the carpet set to the front of the vehicle. What luxury, will this dash my hopes of off-roading KYJ? It's about time we started some finishing touches to the inside. This set of carpets was supplied through the trade by PWB Replacement Motor Parts.

They were simple to fit, using an aerosol of trim spray to secure the material to the faces of the seat box, outside edges and centre of the bulkhead. A sharp Stanley knife was all that was required to trim off the surplus after sticking back. The tunnel and floor pieces were not secured to facilitate taking out for drying.

Now we are back in the workshop. Darren fits a new pair of front lamp grilles, resecures one or two wing stays which have come adrift over the years and fits a new pair of rear mudflaps whilst I start preparing to Waxoyl the chassis.

Now I'm really into Waxoyl, as it's been used for years and years for all the Land Rovers I've owned. And it definitely works. Remember me telling you that the chassis nearly always rusts from the inside out. So where have you got to spray it? You guessed right. It needs to be well applied to the whole of the inside of the chassis. That's why we drilled all those extra holes.

Just as I go to set up the gear, it clouds over and becomes chilly. Typical. When applying Waxoyl, you really could do with a warm day as the Waxoyl needs to be thin enough in the can so it sprays easily.

If the temperature is cool one can simply thin the Waxoyl by immersing the can in a bucket of boiling water. You'll need to hold the can down with a heavy object otherwise it will float.

Now I've been using the same old spray lance that I've owned for fourteen years which is when I first refurbished Sybil (SYB 617) the Series One I own. Back all that time ago Finnigans, who make Waxoyl, used to supply a small DIY lance and I expect they still do.

But as I've got my airline lance and have the use of a workshop compressor, I will use that as I need to inject ten litres worth into every nook and cranny of that chassis in a short space of time. I'm not having it rust again after putting in so much work.

My method is to concentrate on one section at a time starting with a main chassis rail. Working from front to back, then back to front injecting the Waxoyl through every hole along its length with one eye looking at the hole ahead checking that it's running through and spraying out. If the lance you use doesn't reach in far enough then attach a piece of tube on the end to reach in further.

Naturally all the time I am wearing goggles and a mouth and nose mask and it's not long before Darren throws all the doors wide open and goes and finds another job outside whilst I finish.

Then it's onto the crossmembers, each in turn, working from each side. As I get to

Δ *Applying the underseal, not too thick, not too thin, a nice even coating is required. It deadens panel vibration, as well.*

◁ *A simple method of holding new mudflaps in place whilst drilling holes*

the last crossmember I work back along them again only this time giving the outside a spray over, especially the tops which may have missed out on some paint. And so onto the chassis rails themselves, bringing in at that stage all the other items of metalwork like stays, brackets and mountings.

Finally, just to make sure I've not missed a single part, I start all over again and do just the same. No way will rust occur now.

The fumes settle whilst I clean out the lance and tubes with gunwash. The goggles are cleaned, the nose well blown and the disposable mask is burned. The satisfaction is building up, not far to go now with this anti-rust treatment.

Darren and James come in to inspect and nod for approval. James enquires. "What are you going to do now"? I reply "I'll underseal it whilst it's clean and dry."

As I prepare to underseal, Darren finishes off the fitting of the mudflaps and lamp grilles.

James reckons to use four litres of Panel Guard for undersealing a SWB Land Rover. It's quite thick, so I thin each with a little thinners, filling the containers to the top. The caps don't actually screw on. So care must be taken when shaking the canister by holding down the cap.

With a fresh mask, clean goggles and well Waxoyled overalls, I underseal each wheelarch at a time using about half a litre for each. To make sure I haven't missed anything a lamp is used to check behind the bodypanels as all is darker and dingier than ever now.

I then work along the floor under the backbody, then under the door sills and up and around the bulkhead. After constant inspection with the lamp I then take in the new fuel tank and finish up what's left on the chassis.

Gunwash is used to clean off the small amount of overspray on the exhaust system and bodywork.

Now she really is looking good underneath. James exclaims: "Well David, I hope you never ask me to weld anything onto that chassis, with all that preservative in it and on it!"

KYJ still isn't finished by any means yet. There's all those fiddly little jobs which are going to take a few more days yet, but not needing workshop facilities.

By the time you read this I hope that she will have passed her MOT with flying colours. Although no doubt my fingers will be crossed when I take her back to Winston Pincombe for the Test where we bought her.

As yet I've not driven KYJ once on the road during the twelve months LRO has owned her. I look forward to doing that soon and reliving the many, many years that my wife Tina and I have used Series I, II and II vehicles.

And, by using her daily, very soon I'll get to finish those little jobs which will make her even more satisfying to drive.

My grateful thanks to James and Melanie Tennant, Four Wheel Drive Specialist, Corda Farmhouse, Sourton, Okehampton, Devon EX20 4HW (Tel. 0837 86478) for the use of their workshop facilities. And to James for his guidance, help and expertise.

But a special thanks to Darren Phare, James's apprentice, who more often than not worked alongside me, often teaching me a thing or two and was never camera shy when I snapped away.

△ *Fully refurbished into a fine example of a classic Land Rover*

On the road

AS I START writing this last part I'm really excited because tomorrow morning I shall be driving KYJ for the first time, to take her for the MOT at Winston Pincombe's Garage in Chulmleigh.

NO DOUBT your eyes have already scanned the pictures here showing KYJ in all her glory. My, it's been a long time since we started, and it makes me feel good to show her off for the first time.

Before I go any further let me tell you about what I've been doing to the vehicle during this last month.

First job after transporting KYJ back from James Tennant's facility on our trailer was to give both the engine bay and exterior bodywork a jolly good clean up. It must have been last April since I attacked the grime under the bonnet and the body was resprayed at the end of May.

Since then, the Land Rover has been in and out of James' workshop like a yo-yo. And of course we took it to Billing Aquadrome last June for the LRO Weekend Gathering. During this time, what with all the work being done and being parked out in the open, the dust and dirt had well and truly got trapped into every nook and cranny. The spraying of the chassis, waxoyling and undersealing couldn't have helped either, for the bodywork was literally covered in black spots.

Still no problem, I sprayed neat Jizer all around under the bonnet and over all the bodywork, followed by a good rinsing down with the jet of the powerwasher. Still it wasn't really clean, so I then attacked the whole area again with neat Truck Wash detergent with the lance and let that sink in for a few minutes.

After a thorough rinsing down with the powerwasher, that did it. Just goes to show your vehicle is easier to look after if you clean it more often than every nine months. The bodywork still needs a careful rubbing down with T-Cut and a good waxing, so when you next see some pictures she should look even better.

As this last week's weather has been particularly good I decided to put other things to one side and take advantage of the sun. After all since when has the last week of February been better than our average summer?

Off with the bonnet, and off came every bit of metalwork that I could unscrew from the engine in order to rub down each item prior to painting. Just as I like using waxoyl, I like using smooth Black Hammerite, so each item got a hand brushed coating of the latter as you can see from the pictures.

Next, my attention turned to the interior. What a mess. Although we fitted the carpet set for the benefit of the Billing event the rest looked 'tatty' to say the least.

First job was to finish stripping out the old door trims and rub down the surrounding bodywork in preparation for giving two coats of Marine Blue paint by hand.

Some time ago we acquired a full set of replacement door trims from PWB Re-

Break down components like this as much as possible before painting. ▷

What can't be taken off easily, paint in situ ◁

placement Motor Parts Ltd of Warwick to smarten up the interior. These replacement sets come all prepared in three sections for each door. After scratching my head on where to start I decided to loosely screw with self tappers a fixing in each corner of the bottom panel.

I then made diagonal cuts in the vinyl covering the slot that goes over the window latch hole in the upper panel, folding the 'envelope' through the slot and glued the tucks to the back of the zinc panel. The reason that this is not done for you is, of course, to allow one to use the same panels on the door of a series two — which doesn't have the same type of window catches.

This upper panel simply hooks over the bottom window glass surround and is secured into place with a self taper in each bottom corner, and I fitted one in the centre as well. Before finally securing, take back off the bottom panel, offer the armrest into place with the top corner tags that clip under the top panel. Finish drilling through those tags and secure.

Now offer up the bottom panel again, marking the position of the holes for the door pull handles, then secure the panel into place. Mark out with a ruler equally spaced holes along the bottom and up each side at approx 5"-6" intervals, drill and finish securing with self tapers.

Noting where you marked the original holes for the doorpull, move those marks one way or another just ½", using the handle as a guide and re-drill to allow for the largest, or rather fattest, of self tapers that you can lay your hands on that fit through the holes in the handle. As far as I can see this is the best way of refitting the handles. Or you could use speednuts over the metal lip. This is unless someone out there has got a better idea.

Here's a couple of tips. I managed to find a supply of black self tapers to secure those panels. Looks quite smart. The other tip is, when drilling the holes for the screws, place a washer with a small centre hole over the drill bit. Because you probably have one hand on the door and holding the drill in the other, it's too easy to have the chuck damaging the vinyl surface as the drill breaks through.

Next job was to clean the headlining in the front of KYJ (I'll worry about the back later), the sunvisors, dash, parcelshelf, steering wheelk and all the gear sticks. For this I used Amway 'LDC' cleaner diiluted with water about 50/50, using a nailbrush to get into the grain. To finish off when dry, I used an aerosol product called Back to Black for all the black vinyl areas.

There were some splits in the dash and the only thing I could think of to deal with these was to use some of my black tank tape which we use for waterproofing.

The window glasses all around the vehicle both inside and out were given a 'sparkle' by using some Amway 'See Spray' glass cleaner.

After masking off the white button on the ▷

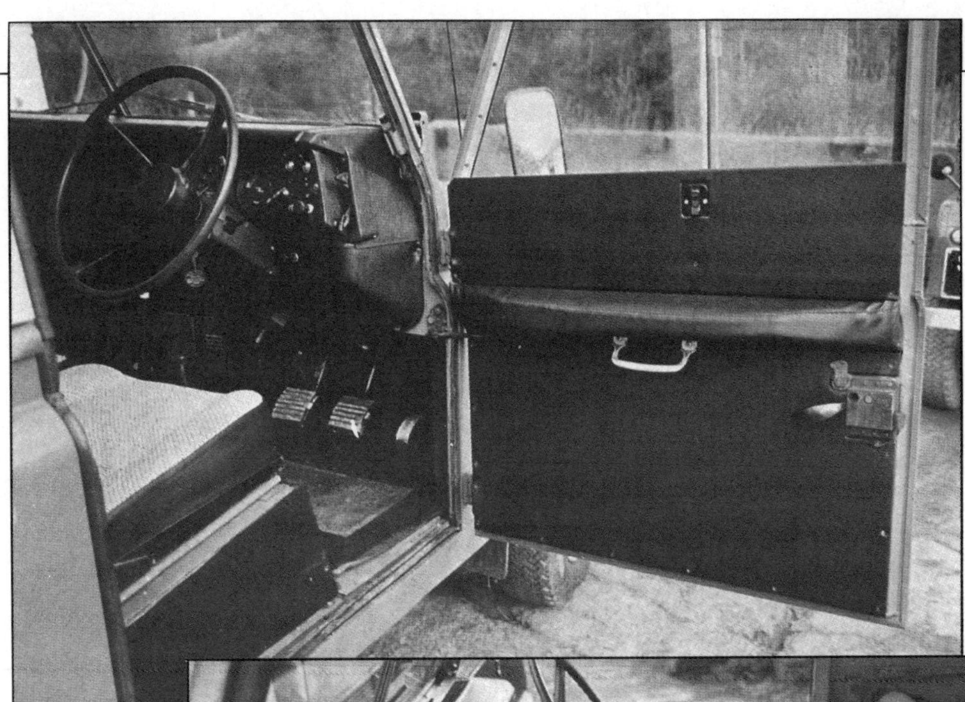

The new door trim in place to complement the recently carpeted interior

Comfortable new seats, a great improvement over the old split vinyl originals

handbrake, I lightly rubbed the old worn paint down and gave a coat of Hammerite, likewise the main gearstick and foot pedals got similar attention.

As the day ticks by, KYJ is looking smarter by the minute inside. The grand finale was to take the clear plastic covers off the seat swabs and backs. You'll remember that I fitted the new replacement seats for the Billing Show.

The original black vinyl seats were in a disgusting state when we bought KYJ and there was nothing we could do with them. We decided after looking at various options of replacing with either standard (not very exciting) or deluxe black vinyl seats (still not very exciting) or to go for cloth finished seats. Talking this through with James, he commented: "You know that PWB Specialist Motor Parts do them don't you."

Well, of course they do! In fact I'm sure about the only thing they don't supply for Land Rover is the axles, transmission and engine! And that goes for Range Rover as well. I must find time to visit this company at Warwick, I understand from their Tim Pickering that they employ some seventy people and that their order books are bursting at the seams with regular orders from Land Rover and Range Rover dealers from both the UK and abroad.

The seats as you can see from the pictures, are PWB's county style cloth seats in grey caviar tweed (they make brown brushwood tweed also). They are very smart, should be warm in winter and cool in summer. When we go off roading in KYJ I'll find a way of protecting the surface to keep mud and water off. Though I should think the surface should clean easily using one of the new fangled aerosol dry cleaning concoctions that you can get these days.

Well, apart from doing general sundry minor jobs like tightening the odd loose screw, painting the number plate light and the Land Rover oval badge opposite, that's about it for this month. I still have the job of preparing and hand painting the whole of the inside of the back of the vehicle.

Now it's Friday morning, day of the MOT. Up early, put a set of tools in the back (you never know) but mainly to include bottle jack, operating lever and wheelbrace.

In an envelope I carry the motor vehicle insurance cover note, the vehicle's registration document and a cheque made out to Post Office Counters Ltd for £100 in order to get the road fund licence — today! How's that for confidence. All I need is a new MOT Certificate.

Remember, I haven't driven KYJ at all on the road since we've had her. I've only been a passenger a couple of times while James has been road testing with trade plates attached.

Off we go, it's about twelve miles up the Barnstaple road to Winston Pincombe's garage at Chulmleigh. As I leave our potholed farm track onto the tarmac there's me thinking very quickly, 'This goes well'.

◁ *Norman Greenslade checking under the vehicle during the MOT test*

Checking the exhaust for excessive harmful emissions ▷

Up our steep hill into the village (one in three on the first bend) and she pulls like a dream in second. Out of the village onto the main road and within seconds I'm looking for fifth. Brain tuned to 5-speed boxed Ninety! No problem, dropped into overdrive top and we sail along. Makes you feel good buzzing away at just 50, lovely morning, feeling of spring in the air, driving a little of Britain's Heritage.

We are soon at the garage. Winston Pincombe's garage is a huge place, you could lose a dozen vehicles inside easily. The doors are open, so I simply drive right in.

Well, talk about putting a smile on your face, as I shut the ignition and get out, I'm surrounded. A good seven, mechanics (or perhaps that should be Land Rover technicians) clamber into her, around her, under her and heads under bonnet.

Then it dawns on me, they must all read LRO! They were all genuinely interested in how KYJ turned out. For you newer readers, we bought this typical Series III from this garage just over a year ago as a total MOT failure, looking very bedraggled having spent its previous year as a hard working farm runabout.

Mr. Pincombe's offer when we bought her was to MOT her after the work was completed. When he made that offer there was a definite glint in his eyes because he knew that we took a fair task on.

Then he and his wife, Heather came from the office, no doubt worrying why the workshop had gone quiet. They too were pleased to see the results. With them was one of their clients, an owner of a One Ten calling in for a service and he too had been following the series.

Winston says, well let's get her over to the MOT bay and introduced me to Norman Greenslade their MOT tester.

Well, I think you can guess, KYJ passed with ease on every single count because we made sure that there wasn't a chance of failure.

It was very interesting watching Norman going about his profession, methodically checking over the vehicle. Interesting because everything he checked, we had done too when originally reporting upon the condition of the vehicle to establish what needed doing.

For testing the brakes he backed the Land Rover off the ramps taking the back and front axles in turn over the rolling road. Checking the exhaust emission was enlightening, too, as he kindly explained what he was doing and what results he expected.

I quote from the MOT Handbook two paragraphs as applicable to our vehicle which was first registered 22nd September 1975:–

Exhaust Emission, Reasons for Rejection:–

A vehicle registered on or after 1st August 1975 which has a hydrocarbon content in the exhaust gas exceeding 1200rpm for a continuous period of 5 seconds. (On the digital readout ours registered 174).

 ▷

The completed engine bay, looking like new

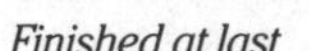

Finished at last

On the road to a new life

A vehicle registered on or after 1st August 1975 which has a carbon monoxide content in the exhaust gas exceeding 6% for a continuous period of 5 seconds. (Ours registered 3.68%).

We were well within the limits. At the end of the test I asked Norman how LRO readers could ensure their vehicle was within limits. No problem, he said, service the engine methodically before the MOT test. Fit new plugs, fit new points, change or clean the various emission valves, but above all else set the engine up in accordance with the manufacturer's data. It's all down to servicing on a regular basis.

With that he proceeded to write out the Test Certificate.

After a cup of coffee with Norman and his colleagues it was goodbye and thanks to Mr & Mrs Pincombe. I drove straight to the Post Office in Crediton to tax the vehicle. During the last week I've used her daily whenever possible.

Well, that's more or less wound up this series on refurbishment. I've learnt much about the work in hand and have gained confidence in doing so and I hope you have done too in the work you have carried out on your vehicles.

The subtle difference between refurbishment and restoration is that doing the latter you strip down the vehicle completely and carefully inspect, repair as necessary and repaint every single item as you build from the chassis up. We couldn't do that as we needed to either push or drive the vehicle out of the workshop each day as it's only been worked upon for an average of two days a month since April.

I might, however, sort out my own workshop at the Centre so the next project will be 'Restoration'. Well perhaps next year.

Next month, especially for those of you who are new to Land Rovers, I will give you my impressions of using our Series III. This will be followed by a series of fitting guides. We will fit side windows, rear seats, free wheel front hubs, an electric winch, CB radio and whatever else comes to mind. You can be sure to see KYJ at the shows this year and I intend using her getting up to various tricks which I'm sure you'll read about.

My thanks to Tim Pickering of PWB Replacement Motor Parts Ltd., 11-13 Warwick Industrial Estate, Budbrooke Road, Warwick CV34 5XH. Tel: (0926) 494782, original supplier (trade) of the chassis sections, body panel sections, fuel tank, window sections, carpet set, door trim and seats.

Thanks too, to Winston Pincombe, The Garage, Chulmleigh, Devon. Tel: (0769) 80900, for supplying the vehicle and carrying out the MOT. He has a super selection of Land Rover, Range Rovers, Ifor Williams Trailers, a few Discoverys and offers a good service in spares and servicing.

Finally my grateful thanks to David Knight, long time friend who so kindly prepared and resprayed KYJ to make her a rather special vehicle.

By David Bowyer

KYJ comes back to life

HAVING SPENT 10 months of odd days bringing our project vehicle 'back to life' I can honestly say I have really enjoyed using her both on, and off road. Throughout the seventies and eighties our family used regularly every day either a Series II or III Land Rover. There was nothing you couldn't do with a Land Rover. Our three children grew up with them.

Every year we would tow the caravan on holiday to either Wales or somewhere else in the country, tow a horse box to shows and events or hook a trailer on the back to move 'you name it' for everyone in the village. Amongst our local community we used to cut and fetch logs every year between six of us lads. And a load was always a good two tons.

Then, in the autumn of 1988, I took delivery of my first all singing and dancing coil sprung Ninety V8. Some readers may remember my short series entitled 'Working a Ninety' in the 1989 July and September issues of this magazine. I still have that vehicle, and I enjoy every moment of using it, both on and off the road.

One reason for purchasing one of Solihull's newer breeds was I wanted more comfort, especially for longer journeys and better cross country work, given it's enormous long travel coil springing. It's powerful V8 engine was chosen as I am not a lover of the Land Rover Turbo Diesel unit. Of course, since then we have had the introduction of the now famous TDi and that's a different cup of tea altogether, for it's a brilliant engine.

So, what's it like going back to using a leaf sprung vehicle? Driving KYJ for the first time early last March, I was expecting 'a good drive', 'goes quite well', 'not too bad for a seventeen year old vehicle, considering it's a four cylinder'.

How wrong I was. It drives very well, has plenty of get up and go, and certainly doesn't feel like a well used example with nearly a hundred thousand miles on the clock.

That's what refurbishment is all about. Bringing your older vehicle back to life. Giving it that 'new' feeling. Making the vehicle a pleasure to use again. The interior trim is nice around you, the steering feels right, the brakes work as they were designed to, the clutch takes up nicely, and the throttle responds well. Through the scratchless windows, the bonnet gleams before you.

I hope this is wetting your whistle, because I am delighted with the vehicle in most respects. It is a reward indeed for the past year's efforts.

The beauty of refurbishing a vehicle is that you should be able to use it for everything it was designed to do. And by that I mean, you use it sensibly 'off road'. In the case of a full restoration, every single bolted assembly is taken off, stripped if the slightest wear is present, repaired, repainted and reassembled meticulously to the original specification to a full concours standard. But I wonder how many owners would start using their Land Rover, or Range Rover come to that, from day one after passing the MOT on short journeys, long journeys and in all weather conditions, and within a month take it across the mountains of Wales like we did?

So what have we been up to in the last three months? During the first two weeks I drove KYJ into town and back a few times, just to make sure all was well. I soon found that having no side windows (now fitted) was an absolute pain as several road junctions in the area are not at right angles. Still I soon managed to live with it, after all it was no different to using a soft-top.

My first long journey, I called it my maiden voyage, was all the way to Solihull for the Association of Rover Club's A.G.M. with a visit to PWB's factory at Warwick on the way. That little round trip was nearly five hundred miles. That blew the cobwebs out! And I'm not joking. The mainly motorway journey did the performance of the vehicle a power of good.

As mentioned before, the engine is not original, but a replacement. I have no idea how many miles it has done. All I know is it pulls well from rest on either 205x16 or the larger 7.50x16 tyres, takes the overdrive in it's stride and holds nearly seventy on the motorway.

On mentioning to Tim Pickering of PWB Replacement Motor Parts Ltd that about one of the only disadvantages of using KYJ on the open road was the general din from inside the vehicle. He promptly dived up the stairs in the factory to the trimming area and brought down a large bag of acoustic sound deadening material, exclaiming, 'fit that, it'll make a difference.' Thank you, Tim.

One or two other observations I could make at the moment is that the power of the headlights is towards useless! This is not helped by the fact that the galvanised grilles are partially obscuring the beams. I must look at alternative light units.

I don't like the standard steering wheel. The rim is spindly and cold. Perhaps I will fit an Alexander padded steering glove or give Mr. Craddock a ring as several readers have told me that his range of replacement steering wheels is excellent.

All in all, that first long journey was very uneventful and keeping to a general speed of 55-60 miles per hour, the vehicle drove nicely giving reasonable comfort. PWB's county style cloth seats are definitely very good indeed. You don't slide on them and you don't sweat on them like the good old Land Rover standard vinyl ones.

The next long journey straight after Easter, was a delightful break up in the mountains of mid Wales doing what I like most

when it comes to off roading, travelling ancient byways. This was to be KYJ's first off roading foray. But before going, there was some extra preparation to do.

Our project vehicle needed some decent tyres. The previous few months she had been shod with a set of fairly well worn 205x16 M&S boots. These Michelin tyres are absolutely brilliant for a vehicle such as this. The supple side walls gives a more comfortable drive and as a general purpose mud and snow tread design they are quite suitable for the occasional off road session providing that the conditions are not too muddy, too wet (meaning grassland hills) and not too deeply rutted.

And where were we going? Wales. For as long as I can remember, it always rains at sometime when in Wales. Mud doesn't matter much as the tracks I choose in the area are rocky in the main. Mud baths I'll rather keep clear of, although I enjoy the occasional watersplash. Some tracks however can be very slippery when wet and the tread of the tyres like KYJ had tend to clog quickly and impede forward progress. The other problems is, of course, you don't get good ground clearance under the axle diffs when the vehicle is sat on 205x16s.

The obvious answer was to fit a set of 750x16 boots. The engine certainly seemed good enough to pull the larger diameter tyres. The rims we fitted a few months ago were the wider 5½" which are just wide enough to accept 750s. But what make and at what cost? A set of radial Michelin XCLs would be nice, but at around £100 each — too much. On my Ninety I am using Radial Cooper Discoverers, but again the best price I can get is £85 each. Both prices include VAT.

Keith Hart, my colleague said 'get a set of Super Mud Plugger remoulds from Wales.' a timely reminder, thank you Keith. Because I run three V8 vehicles around us at the Centre I tend to disregard cross ply and remould tyres as they are not rated for V8s. But the project vehicle, why not?

Everyone must surely know that for purely off-road work Firestone SAT (Super All Traction) or similar tread design such as Super Mud Plugger remoulds must be close on the ultimate tyres to have. The grip is phenomenal in wet muddy conditions, they are not too wide as to roll on the surface — in other words they 'bite' the ground. And the side lugs are brilliant for climbing out of most mild ruts. The minus points are that they give a harsher ride and they 'drone' when driven fast on the open road.

On checking with my local tyre dealer Firestone SATs are becoming hard to get — never did find out why. So, as an alternative, I rummaged through the adverts in LRO until I found the principal suppliers of Super Mud Pluggers. The company is Ponthir Tyre Services and I spoke to their very helpful Rob Jeffs. I explained what I was considering.

He said if I was about to cross Africa, then remoulds are definitely out. If I was going to spend all the time on the tarmac, they will wear out quickly. But because I am invariably driving off road (now where did he get that idea from) and it's not V8, the 6-ply Super Mud Pluggers should fit the bill nicely. As a matter of interest, these remoulds are made in Wales.

The price quoted was a very reasonable £45.25 each including delivery and VAT. So I agreed to order five and gave my credit card number. That was midday. The following morning just after 8 o'clock a lorry turned up at the Centre, with the five tyres. That's what I call service. Ponthir Tyre Services address is Unit 3, Boxer Trading Estate, Ponthir Road, Caerleon, Gwent NP6 1NY. Tel: (0633) 420211.

Our local ATS tyre depot supplied five Michelin Airstop tubes, fitted the tyres and balanced the front pair. Since fitting I tend to maintain the tyre pressure at 22psi for off

▷

road work and 30psi on road. Should KYJ be loaded heavily at any time I would increase the rear tyres to 40psi.

Other preparations prior to leaving for Wales was the temporary fitting of a CB radio, borrowed from the Ninety. (In a following chapter I will cover the installing and setting up of a CB unit as a radio set like this is absolutely essential when green laning). I applied a 1mm bead of my silicone grease to the joint between the distributor body and the cap. Sprayed a thin layer of aerosol silicone grease over the distributor cap, HT leads and coil. A wading plug was screwed into the threaded hole at the lower front of the bell housing. As the vehicle had at that stage covered about 700 miles, a good half hour was spent underneath checking the tightness of all 'U' bolt nuts, shackle bolts and nuts, exhaust system and fluid levels.

To finish off the preparation of the vehicle, a comprehensive tool kit, odd parts box, Jackall and plywood base, shovel, gloves, boots, bow saw, macheté together with sundry ropes and shackles all got jammed in around the spare wheel lying in the back, the lot being suitably tied down. Because the Series III only has two rear door hinges it's not fair on them to try and take the weight of a huge 7.50x16 wheel and tyre when bouncing around off road.

Suitably loaded with lots of waterproofs, we leave Devon mid afternoon Easter Monday along with Greg King, my passenger from Salcombe and David (gadget man) Roffey from Newquay following in his ex-RAF lightweight. We join the M5 at Tiverton and before we know where we are, we are travelling in convoy like a demented caterpillar in three lanes of stop, start, slow to half fast in one enormous traffic queue to Bristol made up, I should think, with 95% holidaymakers going home from the West Country. So we nattered on the CB and had a good chin wag about off roading in general.

The traffic eventually clears as we take a short cut from Bristol to the Severn bridge and into beautiful Wales. We reach our pub accommodation high up in the hills above Abergavenny. We are joined by Richard Thomas, our Editor, who arrived at precisely the same time in his ex-MOD lightweight, passengered by ace photographer Chris Bennett.

The following morning we were joined by Larry Byrne in his well known V8 90. His passenger being Gary Newbury, both from Northamptonshire. Without too much time lost we head for the mountains. I lead in KYJ, the Ninety bringing up the rear with, the two lightweights sandwiched in the middle.

When travelling in convoy on narrow roads between the green lanes it pays to spread out with a couple of hundred yards between each vehicle which makes passing vehicles coming in the opposite direction so much easier. This is where the CB proves to be most useful.

Although KYJ was loaded up quite well with the gear and luggage she pulled like a dream, just coughing occasionally on steep hills. Some of those narrow mountain roads have got some very tight hairpin bends.

During the first day we travelled about eighty miles in all, of which 30 miles was pure cross country driving. Virtually all the tracks that day were undulating rocky routes with very few muddy areas to cross, just one or two water splashes. Some ruts in one area were very deep. But as responsible off road users, I can see no reason to deepen the ruts by driving in them. The ground conditions were relatively dry and I believe it makes more common sense to cross moorland areas by driving alongside deeply rutted tracks, on the flat, in such a manner as to hardly leave a mark on the ground. Sometimes it is more appropriate to straddle one of the ruts, but be warned,

▽ *Super Mud Pluggers give a sure grip on most surfaces*

it's easy to fall into it, lop sided!

I am pleasantly surprised by the way KYJ behaved off-road. The engine is superb, for as you are cresting a rise, the revs nicely drop away to save the front wheels spinning and therefore not endangering the half shafts. And then with a little dab of the accelerator pedal the revs pick up again with no spluttering at all.

By the end of the first day I was more than pleased with her. The new road springs we fitted were giving ample axle articulation and with the heavyish Super Mud Pluggers, we rarely had a wheel leave the ground. The ground clearance was more than ample. Two of the lanes had very large rocks scattered all over the show and by picking a route carefully through them, caused very little concern underneath.

Our Editor's lightweight was on the smaller 205x16 tyres and you could hear that clouting the rocks underneath from time to time.

After a pleasant evening staying at an inn in mid Wales we headed north for our second day's off roading. The tracks I used during the middle day include several river crossings. Again the majority of the tracks are rocky which is good because they cannot be damaged, but can be very hard on the vehicle. If for no other reason, driving slowly at probably no more than two or three miles per hour ensures that you don't bounce off the track, you don't wear your vehicle out. And above all, to those looking on, you will give the impression that you, and the small convoy you are part of, are driving sensibly with due regard for other users and the environment. Off roaders gain respect from driving slowly and carefully.

Driving slowly also allows you to enjoy the magnificent views that only Wales can offer high up on the mountains.

I was also impressed with the engine braking when descending down the many rocky tracks. By adjusting the idle stop on the carburettor to 'just enough' to maintain sufficient oil pressure, good engine braking is assured. The Super Mud Pluggers giving 'super' traction when descending with hardly a hint of braking away. When climbing too, the tyres offered remarkable grip, biting all the way. David had similar tyres fitted to his ex-RAF lightweight and he was impressed as well. Larry in his Ninety had SATs fitted so he was one of us, but our Editor's ex-MOD lightweight was only caught a few times on his slightly less aggressive smaller tyres.

Two of our four vehicles were waterproofed against the penetration of water into the high tension. The other two had to use WD40 on more than one occasion when crossing rivers having killed their engines. I'm pleased to say KYJ didn't miss a beat all day having travelled a similar mileage to the day before, but with longer green lanes absolutely miles away from civilisation and tarmac roads.

We finish the day stopping at a hotel I know well, set deep into the hills. The following morning after checking over the vehicles we make tracks again, this time to another range of mountains. We cross rivers, drive across dams, follow edges of reservoirs, drive through forest and cross further mountain passes.

The weather is still dry, but in the forests the ground conditions are wetter. We stick to only routes that are not easily damaged. What's the point in causing damage to tracks? Those tracks can be driven and enjoyed when the weather is better. Makes sense doesn't it? Remember, 'Tread lightly on public and private land'.

One track we used required not only the door mirrors turned in and the windows shut, but the CB aerials taken off completely as the trees had grown so much into the track. But it was fun, the scratching sounded terrible, fortunately no one's paint suffered.

▷

Something that was very noticeable to me was that when traversing rough terrain, there's a lot less slack in the transmission than you get with a full time drive Ninety, One Ten or Range Rover. That made driving off road even more pleasant.

Our last track to finish off this super holiday break was to drive high up into a mountain pass from where you could see lakes up in the surrounding hills behind you and across the coast and sea to the west.

Many miles both on and off road were covered this last day and it dawned on me that KYJ's suspension had been steadily settling with all the off roading. During the first few hundred miles the ride was 'pitchy'. But now she had settled giving a pleasant ride. Obviously, the journey did her good.

One modification I may carry out to our project vehicle is the fitting of a later brake servo unit.

The braking is OK, but I would prefer to have a servo fitted before towing the caravan, horsebox, or large trailer. Secondhand units are available from a number of sources.

Later in the afternoon it started raining. Absolutely typical. Wales wouldn't be Wales if it didn't rain at some time on holiday would it? And that's when we realised we had another fault. Although the heater/demister blower fan works OK, not much air comes out of the vents. I know these units aren't exactly brilliant, but KYJ's are absolutely useless.

There must be a blockage somewhere, another job to do.

The fourth and final evening was spent at the inn where we started, finishing off the holiday break being within easy reach of the M4/M5 for the journey home on the Friday after breakfast.

By the time Greg and I got back to Devon with David Roffey in convoy, we had driven 650 miles. With other journeys since including our trip up to Cannock to the ARC National Rally, KYJ has covered nearly 2,000 miles since her MOT and being put back on the road.

Overall the vehicle has returned a fuel consumption of 19 miles per gallon which is about right, but driving fast and hard, reduced consumption dramatically to about 14mpg. Oil consumption is around a pint to 400 miles.

To be honest, I almost prefer using the project vehicle to my Ninety for my day to day journeys. Why? It drives like a real Land Rover, uses less fuel than the V8 and is always cleaner — the Ninety spends most of it's life on our course! But above all it's satisfying driving her, having done so much work on it.

I hope many of you have enjoyed this photographic series in these last three issues and may like to take to the hills yourself. But just remember, it's your responsibility to know what is the right track and what is the wrong one and therefore illegal to drive.

Using vehicles on unsurfaced roads (Green Lanes) is an emotive subject. There are many organisations which would like to see recreational motor vehicles confined to major surfaced roads. MOLARA (Motoring Organisation's Land Access and Rights Association) believes that all users of the countryside can enjoy their pastime without upsetting others so long as we all exercise a little care and consideration. This code of Conduct is intended to help you gain the most from your recreation and to protect our future access to the countryside.

1. Use only vehicular rights of way, not all green lanes have vehicular rights.

2. Keep to the defined track. Detour only to pass immovable obstructions. Report any obstructions (including low branches) to the highway authority. If the route is not obvious on the ground, ask locally, or check on the maps held at the highway offices.

3. Travel at a quiet and unobtrusive pace and when travelling in groups, keep to a small number.

4. Ensure your vehicle and yourself are fully road-legal. Green Lanes are subject to the same laws as surfaced roads. There is no public right to drive in common land, moorland, sand dunes or beach.

5. Pay attention to the four Ws.

Weather: Do not travel on green lanes when they risk being damaged beyond a point of natural recovery when the weather improves.

Weight: Do not use lanes which may be seriously damaged by the wheel pressure applied by your vehicles.

Width: Do not use lanes which are too narrow for your vehicle. Avoid damage to trees, hedgerows and boundaries.

Winches: Use only when unavoidable your priority should be to avoid damage to trees, walls or the surface while recovering.

6. Respect the life of the countryside. Be courteous to other road users, including walkers and take great care when passing horses. Be prepared to stop your engine if necessary. Always fasten gates and take care near livestock.

7. Remember that wildlife faces many threats and green lanes can be valuable habitats. Take special care in spring and early summer.

In closing, should any readers like to accompany me on one of my future trips through Wales please give me a ring at my Off Road Centre in Devon on (0363) 82666. For your interest we only travel legally driveable byways which have taken several years to research, with a maximum of four vehicles in a group, and only go mid weeks for obvious reasons.

By Robert Ivins

V8 emissions

WITH THE introduction of exhaust gas testings in the MOT test recently, many post-1975 vehicles have been failing for wrong CO readings or high hydrocarbon (i.e. unburnt fuel) in the exhaust. If that has happened to you, or is likely to, now is as good a time as any to solder the poppit valve on the throttle butterfly shut to give a better tickover speed and replace the rubber diaphragms.

If this is then all set up properly a pass is guaranteed and you may get an extra mile or two per gallon.

We shall assume that all the electrical side has been set up and is in good order and properly timed.

Remove the air cleaners and undo the pipes and links to the carbs in turn and remove them one at a time.

Mark the throttle butterfly with a very small punch at the positions 'B' in the diagram to facilitate assembly. Unscrew the screws 'A' and slide out the butterfly. With a blowtorch heat up the brass butterfly and solder the valve 'C' shut.

Reassemble with the dots as marked and test the flap opens and shuts as before and move on to the other carb.

When the carbs are reinstalled take out the four screws which hold the top body on to the carb and lift the top out. Pull out the air valve spring, diaphragm and needle.

Release the four screws and separate the diaphragm from the air valve. Renew the diaphragm, taking care to fit the locating lug in to its slot.

Reassemble and refit: top up the dashpot with engine oil to within about 6mm of the top and replace the dampers.

Start the engine and run until warm. Disconnect the throttle link between the two carbs and with the end of the hose against your ear put the other end into the mouth of the carb. Adjust the idle speed screws until the sound is the same in each carb and the tickover speed is 800rpm. Adjust the link rod until it fits on without opening one carb more than the other.

Run the engine at tickover and test the CO level.

Follow the instructions for your tester. We used the Gunson's Gastester Mk II which was featured in LRO 'on test' in October.

If the reading is higher than the 3-3.5% CO specified for the RR then they will need adjusting. The tool with which to do this is available from most DIY shops. It comes with two ends as there are two types needed, depending on the age of the carbs. Engage the outer sleeve in the air valve and feel it drop into its slot. Hold the top as in the diagram and turn the inner tool.

Clockwise increases the CO and enriches the mixture. Anti-clockwise lowers the CO and weakens the mixture.

Try moving in stages of 1/4 turn. Move both carbs by the same amount.

Check the CO reading again and keep on until it is less than the 4.5% required for MOT and within the 3-3.5% specified.

If you have moved them much, the idle speed will need resetting after which you again check the CO. When these are both right check the mixture is balanced in each carb.

Remove the flame tube from your gas blowlamp and put a piece of plastic hose over the end of the gas jet.

Turn the gas on and introduce gas into each carb in turn. If the engine does not speed up then the mixture is OK or rich; if it speeds up it is weak in that carb, so enrich that side slightly and decrease the other by the same amount.

Check the CO again when you have finished balancing the mixture.

The procedure is a bit tedious but pays dividends when finished. By balancing the mixture, the risk of failing the test due to unburnt hydrocarbons is reduced and, as they are money going down the exhaust, it will repay in more miles per gallon.

If one carb is rich and the other weak, the engine will be less powerful, and waste fuel, but the CO recording – an average of the two carbs – may be correct.

Refit the air cleaners (replace if dirty as they will increase the CO reading) and test.

As I said before, don't bother to set the carbs unless the electrical side is perfect as timing, dwell etc., all affect the way the fuel is burnt.

The couple of hours invested should give you one of the sweetest V8s about! Acceleration like a sports car and the economy of a moped – well, nearly anyway!

Tools needed
3ft length of hose
Gas blowlamp
Solder
Screwdrivers (cross and flathead)
1/2" AF open ended spanner
Stromberg adjusting tool (available from most DIY shops)
CO meter such as Gunson's Gastester

Parts needed
2 x diaphragm
Oil to top up dashpots

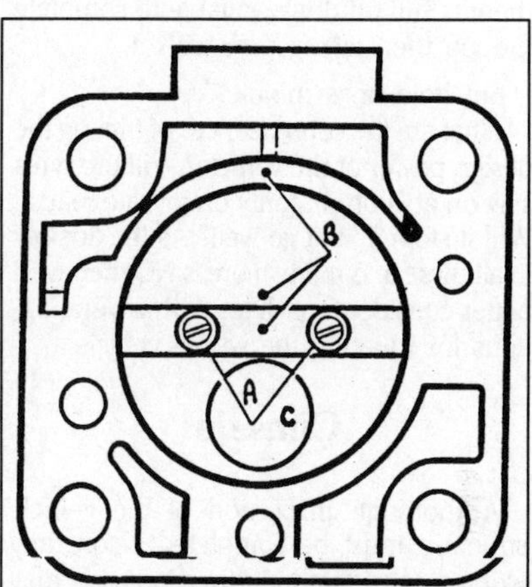

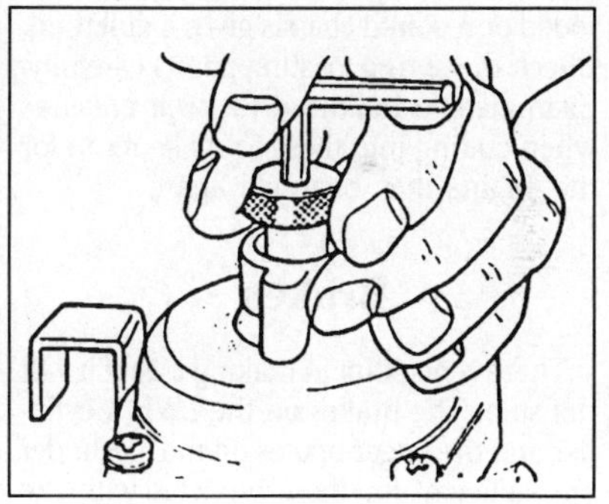

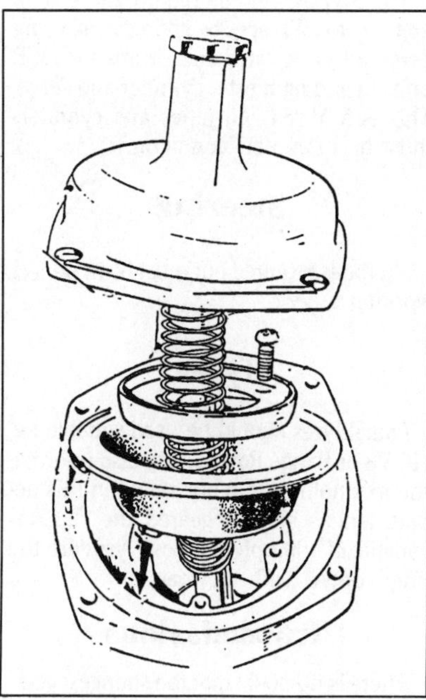

Dropping in a V8

PEOPLE frequently refer to "dropping a V8" into a Land Rover. Many conversions look exactly as if a car engine fell off the engine hoist accidentally into a Land Rover engine bay, instead of being part of a properly engineered vehicle improvement scheme.

The first consideration is to ask your insurance company for a quotation for the finished vehicle. There must be many "two and a quarter V8" engined Land Rovers on insurance company files and on the DVLC computer. If the reply is favourable and there is still funding available to complete the job then let's get on with it.

But hold on a minute.

What are the consequences of tripling the design power of the vehicle? Will the tyres stay on at 100mph (only on private roads). Will it stop? Will it go well? As the answer to all these and many more is NO then we'd better consider a package with several options for uprating the whole vehicle.

Above: V8 showing SD1 flywheel and SII diaphragm

Right: Bulkhead work offside. (The vehicle was rewired later.)

Chassis

A thorough inspection of the vehicle structure must be completed before any work is considered. A "tired" chassis may last several years in normal use but under the extra loading of a V8 may fail in days.

Tap the chassis with a SMALL hammer and listen for a good ringing sound. A corroded or repaired chassis gives a dull thud. Check the spring locating points carefully. Examine the bulkhead footwell areas as when cutting into these to make room for the engine they often fall apart.

Brakes

There is no point in making it go if it will not stop. The brakes on the LWB 4 cylinder and the larger brakes on the 6 cylinder are sufficient for these vehicles with the addition of a servo, unless already fitted. The servo may be the remote type or fitted to the pedal assembly as on later vehicles.

The SWB 88 and 86 require the system uprating to LWB spec by changing all cylinders and backplates and drums for LWB units including master cylinder and servo. This is a MUST. All pipes and cylinders must be in as new condition.

Steering

No mods required but must be in perfect working order.

Tyres

Radial tyres should be used suitable for 110 V8 or Range Rover. They also improve the roadholding. Do not skimp in this department as, suitably geared, the V8 LR is capable of 100mph and your tyres are the only contact with the road.

Transmissions

There is no doubt that the strongest gearbox is the later type series two with the large layshaft bearings and the large intermediate shaft in the transfer box. The series three box will be alright but one has to be careful with the syncromesh on the lower gears as it is not very strong and will not stand hard work.

The gearbox needs no modification other than the addition of an overdrive to increase the gearing. An adaptor plate which is supplied with the conversion kit is used to join the gearbox to the engine.

The axles with standard Rover diffs will cope with the increased power — just!

The LWB series three with its Salisbury rear axle is ideal as the axle is much stronger and will not regularly break half shafts as the Rover axle will unless in gentle hands (feet?). This axle may, indeed should, be fitted to earlier LWB and fits by direct substitution if fitted with a S3 propshaft. The axle may be fitted to SWB if new spring mounting pads are welded on and a new shorter propshaft is professionally made and balanced. If the Salisbury axle is fitted it also has the larger brakes needed fitted already.

New on the market is a conversion by Ian Ashcroft to allow the SD1 5-speed gearbox to be fitted to a Land Rover transfer box. This does not then need an overdrive or engine to gearbox adaptor plate and is a neat looking job. He also makes the same type of conversion for the SD1 automatic gearbox for those who like autos or possibly may need an auto because of disability and cannot afford the many thousands needed for an auto Range Rover. His number is 05827 6081.

Cooling

The standard series three rad will work well with the V8 but needs an electric fan if used with P6 or P5 engines. The standard viscous fan may be used with RR or SD1 engines. The radiator requires the addition of a small pipe soldering to the header tank to take the bleed pipe from the inlet manifold. Do not be tempted to block this pipe off as localised overheating and headgasket failure may result. The SD1 rad may be used with a 110 type front conversion.

Exhaust system

If one has the facilities of a large fabricating shop then make your own by adapting a RR system. If not, then ring Jake Wright who manufactures an excellent set of front pipes which mate to RR manifolds and fits the standard LR system or to his slightly larger bore system which follows the normal routing and uses the original chassis mounts. Ring 0943 863530 for details.

Adaptor kits

Kits are available from many manufac-

Left: Bulkhead work nearside. Note Range Rover type nearside exhaust.

Below: Engine sits in "wide" bulkhead.

turers and vary in price and contents. Some include remote oil filter assemblies, some use an oil pump adaptor and some just use a small oil filter. Some include engine mounts and some you make yourself, but all have a cast aluminium or fabricated engine backplate and flywheel bush and instructions.

Clutch and flywheels

Either the SD1 (P6 "S" is the same) light flywheel or RR flywheel may be used. The slightly rarer SD1 one does not require redrilling to take the LR clutch cover but the RR does. The RR is heavier and gives more lugging ability than the car's.

The standard 9.5" LR clutch plate is used with a S3 cover for a S3 box and RR flywheel. The SD1 flywheel/S3 box uses the SD1 cover or S2 diaphragm cover with its central boss.

With a S2 box then the 9.5" plate is again used with a SD1 or S2 diaphragm cover (LR Part No. 567557). The adjustable mechanism on the S2 clutch being able to cope with both thicknesses of flywheel.

If you use a RR flywheel unless you are skilled in this type of work then have it professionally redrilled and threaded or balanced — related vibrations may result.

A special thinwall spigot bush is needed to fit all conversions.

Engines

One may be forgiven for thinking that all Rover V8 engines are the same. They are basically all similar but have various power outputs and many variations in external fittings such as exhaust manifolds and water pumps, depending on their original application.

All will run on lead-free fuel, the higher compression engines needing retarding slightly. We shall not consider engines from rarer vehicles such as the MGB and LR101 but from more common "donor" vehicles. Try to hear the engine run before purchase. All applications require a RR starter motor as the front propshaft hits the starter solenoid with car type starters.

Rover P5 Saloon and Coupé
Getting a bit old now, but the engine offers lots of power. Was designed to run on now-extinct Five Star petrol but will run on anything if the timing is retarded. Available as an auto only. A RR or SD1 flywheel will also be needed.

Rover P6B 3500 and 3500S
The youngest unit is now fourteen years old but still offers lots of useful life. The 'S' is manual.

Rover 3500SD1
Probably the best engine for the conversion and the most readily available, from car breakers. Try to find a manual one to use the flywheel. Don't forget to buy the electronic ignition powerpack with the engine.

Range Rover
As lots of diesel conversions are carried out there are many engines available. They already have flywheel and correct starter motor and the angled nearside exhaust manifold so are probably the most economic conversion. The engines tend to be harder worked than the car units so watch condition. They are less powerful than the car engines but have more torque.

110, 90
Less powerful but as per RR engines above.

Fuel injected engines
If you can insure it then great, but carry a spare gearbox with you!

The mixing of the ingredients

Before fitting the engine it is best to uprate the rest of the vehicle in respect of overdrive, tyres and brakes (in case we later forget!). This may be over a long period whilst the vehicle is still in use.

Collect all the bits necessary before starting. Remove the old engine — I find it easier to work with the front wings off. Cut the bulkhead on the O/S level with the steering box mounting plate (see photos) and reweld to allow room for the back of the engine.

Repeat on the N/S level with the bulkhead support bracket and reweld. This allows plenty of room for future spark plug changes!

Assemble the clutch and flywheel and bolt on the adaptor plate. Instal the engine into the engine bay.

Fit the exhaust system and make up pipes and connections for the fuel system. The SD1 and later type RR engines need an electric fuel pump mounting on the chassis near the tank. Use the Facet type from the RR or an SU from such as the Jag XJ6. The SD1 pump is actually in the fuel tank and will not fit in the LR. Use RR throttle cable on modified linkage.

Move the battery under the passenger seat and make all the electrical connections. Don't forget a good earth cable between engine and chassis.

Refit the rad after soldering a small copper tube into the header tank to take the manifold bleed pipe and connect to the engine. Depending on your engine/rad type, modify SD1 or RR hoses to fit clear of the fan and belts.

Fit the remote oil filter adaptor. The RR air cleaner is best to use on all engines but the SD1 will fit with RR "elbows'.

Refit the bodywork and try the engine. Check the operation of the clutch before fitting the floor on S2 boxes as it is easier to adjust with the floor missing. The floor will need trimming to suit the modified footwells.

Time now for testing after checking for leaks etc. Remember with twice the power you can get into trouble twice as quickly!

The fitting has been only briefly outlined as it varies with different engine and vehicle combinations. The conversion kits carry good fitting instructions.

By Tim Webster

△ *Rear radius arm has two bushes, it's the one at the axle end which causes most problems.*

The rear suspension A frame. ▷

△ *Front radius arm bushes deteriorate as the miles clock up.*

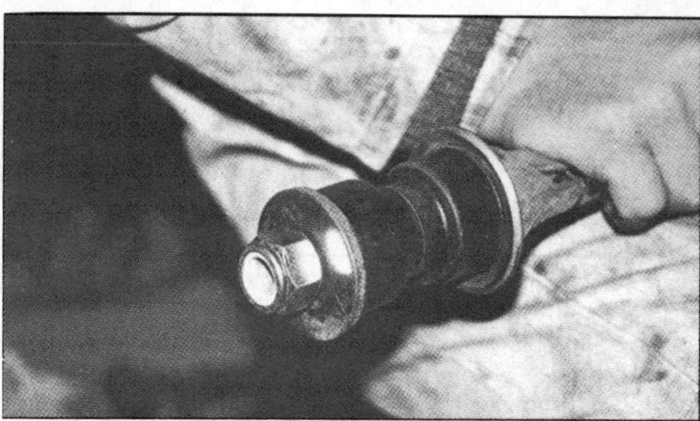

New bushes can be hand-fitted to the front radius arm/chassis pick up point. ▷

Re-bushing

RENEWING the suspension bushes on a coil-sprung Land Rover is a regular chore that many of you might be tempted to tackle yourselves. But, warns Tim Webster, it's not always a straightforward job.

OUR NINETY, a much loved (but frequently hard used) vehicle, was certainly beginning to feel its age when the magic 100,000 miles registered on the odometer at the end of last year. Off-road, the suspension thumped and banged relentlessly, and on-tarmac, its ability to corner in a detectably crab-like fashion told its own story - the suspension bushes were long overdue for renewal.

Those of you who own a Ninety, One-Ten or Range Rover will probably be familiar with all this. Land Rover's coil sprung suspension design gives wonderful compliance, but at a price. And that price is numerous rubber bushes that eventually deteriorate, introducing large amounts of 'give' at axle location points.

In the early stages, bush degradation is largely an audible problem. The front and rear axle radius arms, already working hard under normal conditions, bang against their location points, and the ball joint on the rear axle 'A' frame gives a similar thump when drive is taken up. So, as the condition of the bushes worsens, so too does the quality of axle location, and ultimately the steering becomes vague with the rear axle capable of actually 'steering' the vehicle from the back as it shifts fractionally out of line.

The only solution to this is to renew the bushes, a fairly major undertaking that includes systematic removal and replacement of radius arms, front panhard rod and 'A' frame ball joint. Simple enough in theory, but is it a DIY job that most owners could tackle?

The answer has to be yes, but only in part'. Removal of the suspension components is straightforward enough, as long as care is taken and the vehicle is adequately supported. But even the most enthusiastic owner will probably have enormous prob-

Δ *Front radius arm/chassis pick up point bushes, old and new. Right hand bush has lasted 30,000 miles but has now 'spread'.*

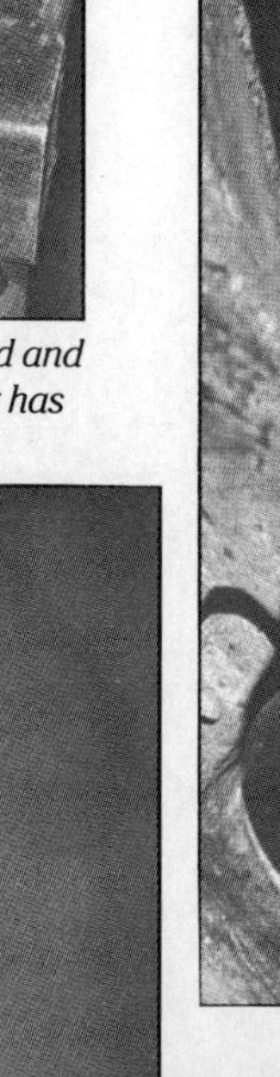

Above: Front radius arm bushes. The left one shows how badly they deteriorate.
Above right: It makes sense to renew the shock absorbers and shock absorber bushes at the same time. These shock absorbers are Genuine Parts, replacing units that lasted well over 60,000 miles. Fitting takes 30 minutes each side at rear/60 minutes at front, if all comes apart easily. Chassis is being refurbished by wire brushing and painting with proper synthetic Chassis Black. Hammerite or Smooth Hammerite is not suitable as it is not oil, petrol or diesel resistant.
Right: New, Genuine Parts 'A' frame ball joint and dust jacket/seal.

a Ninety

lems drifting out the old bushes and fitting new. So much so that, for safety's sake, one should always make provision for professional help and not hesitate to use it if the going gets tough.

To illustrate the point, we decided, as part of a near-total rebuild of our Ninety, to try our hand at renewing all the suspension bushes on a DIY basis. After all, preparing a Ninety for overland travel and not being able to tackle most repair jobs yourself is fairly pointless. So the first task was to study Land Rover's parts manual and order the items required.

As we'd already renewed springs and shock absorbers, we decided to renew all bushes, bolts, nuts, washers and thrust plates, so that the Ninety would end up with brand new suspension throughout. Since we'd heard that most non-Genuine bushes tend to break up very quickly indeed, we decided to use the correct Land Rover items. Land Rover Parts not only got what was quite a hefty order right first time, but also delivered all non-stock items to our local dealer by the next day - bang on time, and a good demonstration of Land Rover Parts being as good as its word; other vehicle manufacturers' parts organisations could learn a lot from LRP!

We checked everything carefully against our list of part numbers, confirmed nothing was broken or damaged, and began the task of removing the Ninety's suspension components. Straight away, we proved (for interest only) that the Ninety could stand, unsupported, with either the front panhard one, one front radius arm, one rear radius arm, or the 'A' frame removed. However, FOR SAFETY'S SAKE, we would advise against doing this without supporting the vehicle on adequate axle stands, and indeed ours remained firmly perched on stands throughout the operation - we'd advise anyone else to do the same.

Once the suspension items were off the vehicle, we could see just how bad the old bushes were. For those unfamiliar with these bushes, the ones that are pressed into the radius arms at their 'axle end', into both ends of the panhard rod, and are used at

▷

△ To drift out old ball joint, the 'ears' of the bolt plate are cut off with a hacksaw. This allows the joint to sit on a brace without fouling the sides when it is pressed out.

▽ . . . as shown below.

Once the balljoint is drifted out, you can see the splines that help give an interference fit with its holder. It's these, not just the bolts that hold it in place. The new ball joint is pressed in, above, with a suitable sizeld hollow drift.

the chassis end of the 'A' frame arms, have a cylindrical steel 'jacket' in which is the rubber bush and a further, much smaller tube through which the bolt passes.

In new condition, the rubber and tubes are firmly bonded together; our old one showed that the rubber gets very brittle over high mileages, parts company with both tubes between which it is sandwiched, and can actually break up and fall away - small wonder they bang away off-road! Replacing these means pressing out the old bush, and pressing in a new item - a problem on a DIY basis.

The bush 'pads' used at the chassis ends of the radius arms also break up, and at best 'spread', so lessening their damping qualities. However, unlike the other bush type, these are simple to replace since they literally bolt in place, and require no special skills.

Conversely, the ball joint on the 'A' frame simply wears out and becomes slack. Its replacement is a complete pre-assembled unit, and needs to be pressed into its collar type retaining bracket and then bolted. Again, we saw this as a potential DIY nightmare.

It was at this stage, we started looking at the options we could use to drift out old bushes ('A' frame ball joint included) and press in new ones. Burning them out was one option, but didn't really help with pressing in the new ones. This, we supposed, could have been achieved with a large workshop vice, but since we didn't have one hefty enough, it would be a sizeable addition to the cost of rebushing. So we took some professional advice, and opted for a local workshop which, equipped with a hydraulic press, took out our old bushes and pressed in the new ones for £20.

It was £20 well spent since, apart from getting all bushes replaced in a few hours, we picked up some well-meaning advice that DIYers should take into account before trying all manner of home-brewed solutions to shift stuck bushes.

The first is that many are tempted to use oxy-acetylene equipment to burn out old bushes, rather than handheld blow torches. The end result can be accidental damage to the radius arm itself which can

Δ *Refurbished 'A' frame on the chassis.*

Δ *Pressing out the front radius arm bushes.*

Front radius arm bushes. A light oiling helps ease them ∇ *in, but must be wiped away to prevent contamination*

become brittle through over-heating and even slightly melted around the edge of its holes. We were also told that using a vice or homemade tools made from bolts and spacers to press in the new bush can end with the bush becoming distorted; it might go in, but the bonding of the rubber will soon fail and replacement might be required in as little as a thousand miles.

The second tip is that the 'A' frame balljoint should always be pressed out with a press, and refitted with the same method. It is possible to drift out the old balljoint manually, but to do this, you should cut away the bolt lugs on the old balljoint, so that the collar type bracket can be adequately supported while you do so. Fail to do this, and you can end up with a fractured or split collar bracket. And since the ball joint is held in place through friction and not by the two bolts, the ball joint can come apart when on the vehicle with predictable results.

A third tip is that manually drifting out the 'A' frame balljoint is not always possible. Some are then tempted to burn it out with oxy-acetylene, and here there is real danger. Within the balljjoint is a highly tensioned spring which, as you burn through the casing, has a tendency to let go in a big way. The possibility of serious injjury should this happen is very high.

Finally, a worthwhile tip is that, with all the bushes in place, refitting the suspension components is an hour or so's work, but it's important only to 'nip' up the bolts until the full weight of the vehicle is taken on its suspension. Only then should you torque up the bolts fully. Fail to follow this procedure, and your new bushes will have a very limited life.

With all new bushes in place, we found the improvement to the Ninety was remarkable. Gone was the banging, thumps and vague steering and, allowing for the vagaries of the Firestone SATS we use on the machine, the precision of the Ninety over all sorts of terrain was back with a vengeance. Replacing all the bolts and nuts – most of which were corroded or noticeably worn - also gave us peace of mind and some reassurance that undetected spoilt threads wouldn't make future re-bushing any more difficult than it need be.

Cost-wise, the best quote we had was £200 for the work alone prior to deciding to do as much of the work ourselves as possible, so going the DIY route certainly saved us a lot of money. But we firmly believe that using some professional help for the harder parts made the whole process easier, quicker and safer, and would strongly urge others contemplating this sort of job to examine their resources and capabilities before committing themselves to doing everything on a strict DIY basis.

WORN "A' FRAME BALL JOINT

Symptoms: Deep thump as drive takes up, delay in drive take up, loud bangs as axle moves (most noticeable over rough ground). Deep thump when braking sharply, rear axle steer.

WORN FRONT PANHARD ROD BUSHES

Symptoms: Vague steering, bangs when steering on high grip surface. At standstill or low speed, excessive sideways axle movement, banging over rough ground

WORN FRONT RADIUS ARM BUSHES (axle end)

Symptoms: Vague steering, banging over rough ground, delay in drive take up (axle twists about its axis)

WORN FRONT & REAR RADIUS ARM BUSHES (Chassis end)

Symptoms: Bangs over rough ground, when braking, when accelerating, rear axle steer, vague steering, tramlining.

NOTE: Important not to confuse above with shock absorber bush failure or steering joint wear. Also check first for excessive differential backlash and UJ wear.

THE MAGIC BOX

LISTEN in on any "Land Rover talk" and the words "low box", "yellow knob" and "transfer box" are bound to creep into the conversation.

Some people are totally *au fait* with the workings of the internals and totally familiar with the use of the various levers in different situations, for some, however, the gearbox is a magic box under the floor and their only contact is with the main gearlever and, through fear or ignorance, they never use the alternative ratios and drive modes.

This is even more so of Range Rovers with many people buying the vehicles and not knowing how or when to use the extra controls.

There are two main types of gearboxes fitted to Land Rover vehicles, the permanent four wheel drive types as first used in the Range Rover, which, with exception of the 101 and 109 V8 were restricted to leaf sprung vehicles, and the much smaller four speed box as fitted to the original 1948 vehicles and continuing unchanged (except in detail) until the end of the line of the leaf sprung range in 1984.

It is some tribute to the pre-war design department at "The Rover" that their design for a gearbox for the mid-thirties was still in production some fifty years later (their diff design still is, too).

The gearbox is not really one gearbox but two bolted together to form an assembly, the main (primary) being a simple four speed forward and reverse.

The transfer (secondary) box is a two speed gearbox with two drive outputs one of which can be selected to be non-operational for road use in two wheel drive. The secondary gearbox also has facility for power take off at the rear or at the bottom.

The gearboxes can and do suffer from many problems, but, as one seasoned French traveller once said of his Land Rover when he had just completed a major desert crossing with a broken layshaft giving him only fourth high and low, they have "courage" and can continue to travel even when suffering from major breakages.

Whilst outwardly looking similar there are many variations on the gearbox. The early vehicles had permanent four wheel drive with an overrun clutch in the front output housing, this was deleted in 1950, and the box continued largely unchanged until the introduction of the diesel engine which featured a different stud pattern on the bellhousing.

This pattern continued for all four cylinder engine except the i.o.e. four and six cylinders, the pattern is still in use on the Discovery and Defender.

The next significant change was in the mid-sixties when the intermediate gear in the transfer box was given a large bearing as was the layshaft. This box is regarded as the strongest and is most suited to hard work or V8 conversions, bearing in mind the V8 is five or six times more powerful than the original design criteria.

The next change came with the introduction of syncromesh on second gear on the last of the series two station wagons and the series three.

The series three box also had a different clutch release mechanism and sealed for life release bearing. With various updates including a stronger reverse gear assembly the box continued until the early eighties and the coil sprung vehicles.

There are many small production sub groups of the above, such as the "One Ton" ultra low geared ultra heavy duty box, and the two wheel drive only with no low range and the front drive deleted. These were used in military variants in 1958 for the UK, and in the seventies for the Belgian Army.

There are many faults which the boxes are prone to. Unfortunately they nearly all involve removal of the gearbox and a complete strip down. Removal is not a simple job.

First the floor plates have to be unbolted and, if they have been in for a long time, the bolts will be seized. Likewise the seat box.

When these have been lifted clear the gearbox itself can be tackled. The two mounts, prop shaft bolts and bellhousing bolts are next and clutch slave cylinder. After the handbrake is disconnected the box may be lifted out of the passenger door.

Two people and a length of rope facilitate the job if a proper floor crane is not available. DIY people should consider hiring a crane as the lifting space is restricted and it is very easy to hurt one's back whilst lifting the box.

The box is best worked on at bench height. After cleaning and draining the oil, remove the clutch mechanism at the front, followed by the gearbox top after taking off the indent springs and plungers. Note that one of the springs is painted yellow and belongs on the reverse selector.

Remove the nut or bolt at the front of the layshaft and, after removing the three large nuts holding the bellhousing, slip the housing off. Remove the PTO blanking plate and top cover and after straightening the locktab undo the castellated threaded ring which holds the mainshaft into the rear bearing.

A proper tool is available for this but most resort to a hammer and blunt chisel. This is not recommended but it works. The difficulty is retightening on reassembly.

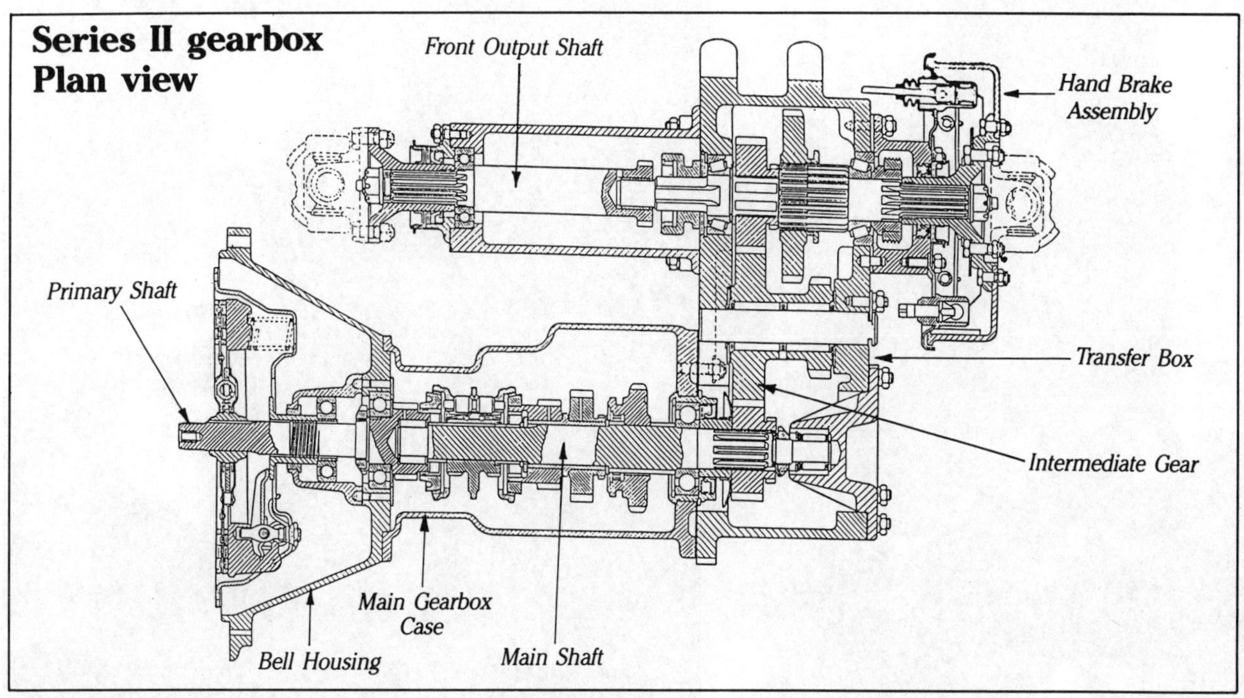

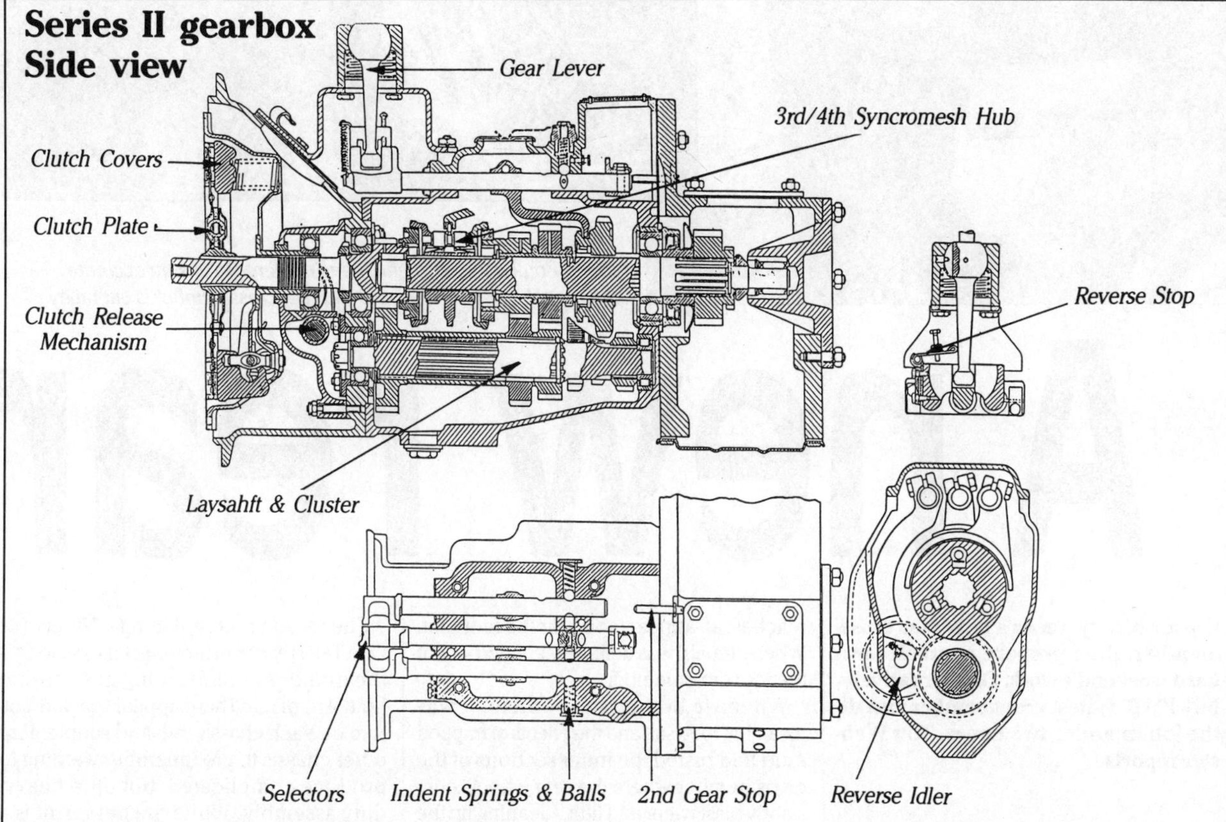

When the selectors have been lifted out the main shaft can be tapped out backwards with a hide or copper hammer. Most problems can now be sorted out at this stage.

Some, like renewing the reverse idler, require the transfer box to be unbolted from the main box. This simply involves unbolting the cases. The transfer idler gear needs removing first as it shields some of the bolts.

Reassembly is the reverse of disassembly. The various workshop manuals cover this in depth and give the various tolerances and settings. Adhere to them for the best results.

Symptom sorter

☐ No drive in first, second or third, but drive in top: Broken layshaft.

☐ No drive in top but drive in first, second and third: Broken mainshaft.

☐ No drive in reverse: Teeth off reverse idler.

☐ Noise in first, second and third but quiet in top: Worn layshaft bearing.

☐ Noise at tickover which goes quiet when clutch depressed: Primary shaft bearing worn.

☐ Jumping out of gear: Worn or damaged synchro or gear, split bronze bush on mainshaft, loose rear mainshaft nut, missing tooth, weak indent springs.

☐ Oil leaks: Faulty seal or gasket or, in exceptional circumstances, a cracked case.

☐ Oil migrating from the transfer box into the main box: faulty inter box oil seal.

☐ Locking up whilst moving: transfer box idler gear bearings breaking up.

These are common faults, there are many more obscure but rarely experienced problems.

When renewing parts use O.E. (Original Equipment) spec. parts as you may labour in vain if you use poor quality components.

As gearboxes go they are relatively simple and may be rebuilt without any special tools, if yours is giving trouble fear not — have a go.

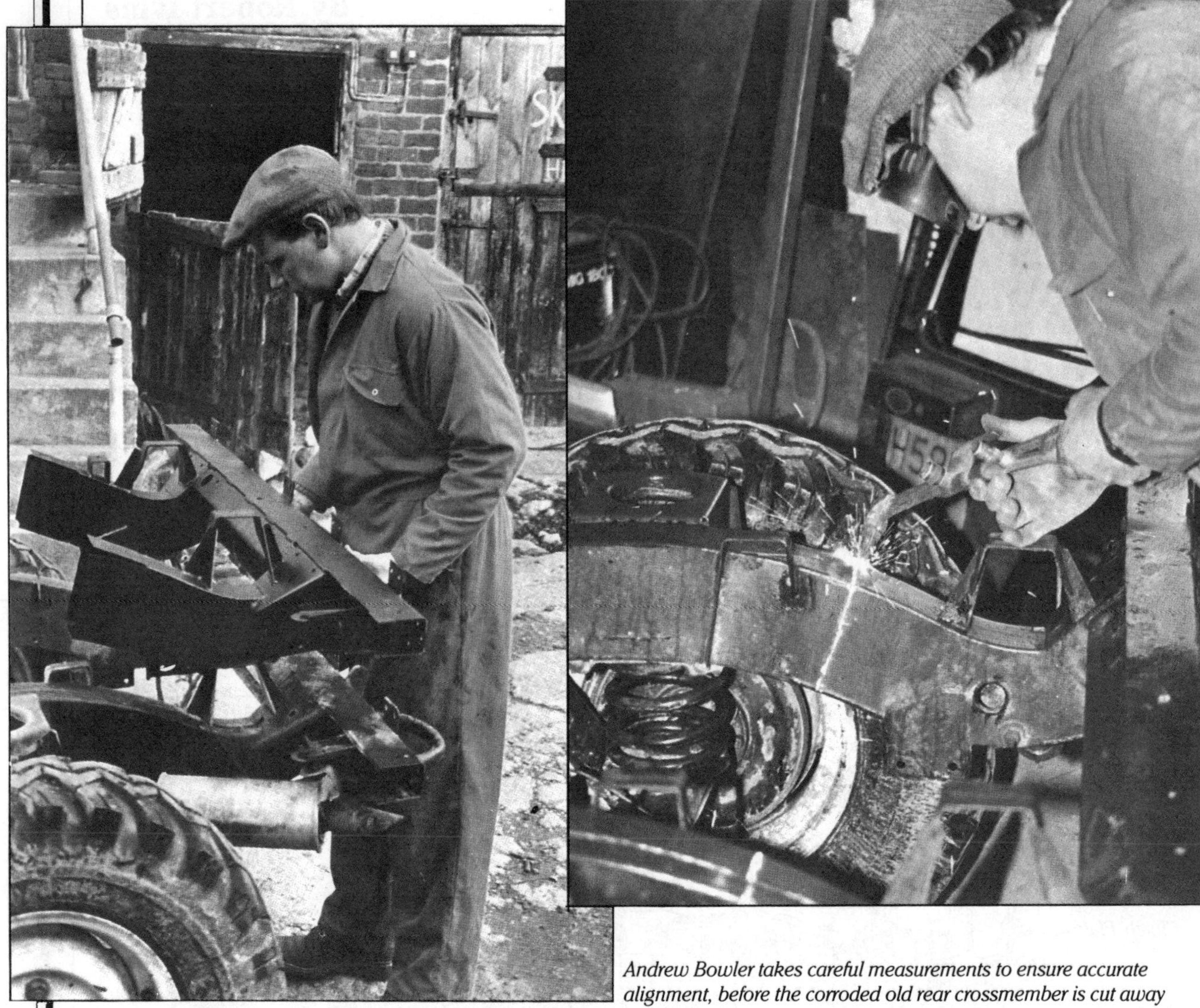

Andrew Bowler takes careful measurements to ensure accurate alignment, before the corroded old rear crossmember is cut away

A new rear

If your Ninety needs a new rear crossmember, then prepare yourself for a hard weekend's work. Or alternatively, buy PWB's latest crossmember and do the job in under two hours. Tim Webster reports.

OUR PROJECT Ninety has spent the last few months in a sorry state of disrepair, following its roll-over last year. Stripped of its bent bodywork, and despite sporting brand new suspension and a host of other newly-fitted mechanical parts, its chassis is nevertheless in need of some refurbishment.

I say 'refurbishment' rather than 'repair', because 100,000 miles and seven years hard use (in the hands of its previous owners) has unavoidably left the chassis liberally coated with surface corrosion, but thankfully there are few areas where welding is necessary.

We did think initially that the front outriggers could be 'shot', but apart from shedding large rust scabs from their inner reaches, all appears solid for the moment. Where 'repair' was definitely needed was at the rear crossmember.

When we bought the vehicle, it was clear that road salt and the effects of trapped mud had rusted the inner sections of the crossmember where the rear wheels constantly blast water and filth. Cleaning up the metal with an angle grinder and industrial wire brush attachment did little to improve matters however, and a stout screwdriver quickly showed up extensive metal perforation – things were far worse than expected.

Given the age and mileage of the Ninety (it is one of the very first 1984 models), we decided that localised repair was false economy, and complete replacement of the rear crossmember was a better option. However, as the Ninety rear crossmember is a far more complex structure than those on earlier models, we braced ourselves for workshop quotes that reflected the predicted solid weekend's work that replacement involved.

The reason that replacing a Ninety (or One-Ten) rear crossmember takes so long is the number of reinforcing gussets that hold it in place. These appear top and bottom on each chassis rail, and supplement other chassis to crossmember welding to produce complicated, but ultra heavy-duty assembly. While the net result is a crossmember equally suited to military and civilian towing work, unpicking all the welds while retaining the condition of the chassis rails is nigh impossible, so a certain amount of fabrication work is normally necessary to complete the job.

Thankfully though, this problem has not gone unnoticed in certain quarters, and PWB Replacement Motor Parts of Warwick has now produced a replacement rear crossmember for Ninetys and One-Tens that includes generous chassis rail extensions.

This in effect is a complete replacement for the very back end of the chassis, and fitting it is a matter of cutting away the old crossmember together with about eight inches of chassis rail, and welding on PWB's

The PWB replacement chassis end. Note fluted ends which slide over existing chassis rails

The new and the old mate snugly ensuring a strong and durable repair

Job done in less than two hours. With bodywork in place it would obviously take longer, but nevertheless, the complete replacement unit makes for an easier life

end

chassis section and crossmember combination. To make the job easy, PWB's extension pieces are also fluted at the ends, so they simply slide over the existing chassis rails, effectively double skinning the repair on all sides of the chassis rails for durability.

The result is a fully fitted replacement crossmember in just under two hours.

Although we we would recommend this new PWB product to anyone with good welding skills and copious DIY enthusiasm, we opted to let Andrew Bowler (of comp. safari fame) fit it to our Ninety. His welding skills are not far short of being an art form in their own right, and bearing in mind the rigours of off-road recovery that the Ninety is often subjected to, we wanted to be sure the crossmember was firmly 'stitched' into place.

As the Ninety is little more than a rolling chassis at present, fitting the PWB crossmember was incredibly simple. Initially, Andrew took time to make copious measurements to make sure the rear body would line up with the securing tabs when refitted. That completed, together with removal of the rear wiring loom which runs inside the chassis, he marked the chassis with chalk 'cut lines' and promptly sliced off the rear of the chassis with an oxyacetylene cutter. Exit the old rear crossmember in just 30 minutes.

The cut ends of the chassis were then dressed with an angle grinder, painted to prevent corrosion getting a hold again, and the entire PWB crossmember assembly was slid onto the chassis rails. We did find that a little trimming was required for the extensions to clear two existing chassis brackets (these may well have been deleted on later chassis – check yours carefully), but after much careful alignment, the first guide MIG welds were made to hold everything in place. Indeed, in just under two hours, all MIG welds had been made, and we had a full chassis again. It's as simple as that.

PWB's crossmember is also extremely impressive in that it is a faithful reproduction of the original. The gauge of mild steel used matches that of Land Rover's, and in every detail, the crossmember is identical. The design of the chassis extensions is also very reassuring, inasmuch as the amount of weld applied during fitting restores the integrity and strength of the chassis rear. This is important to anyone who uses their Ninety for towing work, and is equally so in an off-road situation.

Most importantly, fitting is foolproof, so an adequate standard of repair is more or less guaranteed.

PWB Replacement Motor Parts are now producing rear crossmembers with and without extensions for both Ninetys and One-Tens, and we'd suggest you contact them direct on 0926 494782 to locate one of their dealers near you. In terms of pricing, these crossmembers are so new, dealer prices weren't available at the time of going to press. However, this may have changed by the time you read this, so again contact any of their dealers direct for pricing.

◁ *Removing old runners.*

Slot for Series III Window lock. ▷

Is your Land R

DOOR TOPS

IN MANY people's eyes the Series One was the last "proper" Land Rover. This is very debatable but until the 110, it was certainly the last with "proper" door tops.

The galvanised Series One tops last forever. The thin steel SII/SIII tops don't, and at ten years or so require replacing.

For many years the only tops available were Genuine tops which come fitted with the glass and runners, with a price to match, but the "non genuine" trade had for years been selling a much cheaper bare door top as, after all, the glass seldom rusts!

This prompted genuine parts to supply a bare top as well. Genuine tops 347492 and 3 are about £50. Non genuine, but still aluminium clad as the originals, are just over £20. The window runner is available in 2 metre lengths as each door top needs about 1.7m. One length per door is needed.

The first step after purchase is to paint the top and leave it for a few days for the paint to properly dry. This is not always possible as in the example photographed the top had actually fallen off and the repair had to be immediate so it was painted after being fitted.

As a lot of repairs fall into the "Hospital Job" category at present, i.e. mend it when it falls off, then this will probably be the common way.

Remove the interior trim if fitted and undo the two nuts on the bottom of the two pegs which hold the door top on. These are usually rusted but respond to easing oil.

Be careful not to damage the outer doorskin with the spanner. In an ideal world the top should just lift off but usually needs a flat tyre lever or pry bar to gently ease up the door top bottom rail from the door.

Be careful not to damage the rubber sealing strip.

Place the old top on a flat work surface and unscrew the visible screws in the aluminium glazing strip, unscrew or drill out the window lock and the inter door sealing strip.

Locate the screws which are in the bottom of the window runners and unscrew them. If you tackle the top runner first the glass may be lifted out and out of the way. The remaining runners may then be removed and kept as patterns.

The aluminium packing pieces can now be cleaned up ready to be refitted.

Using the old runners as a pattern, cut the new runner to the exact length needed. The bottom runner on a series III has a slot in it to allow the window catch pin to raise up and lock the window. To cut this slot either drill a few holes with a small drill

◁ *Re-fitting window lock.*

Aluminium strip fitted, door top in place. ▷

over topless?

and trim the excess off or gently grind the slot out with a small angle grinder.

Start fitting the runners in reverse order bedding them in a thin layer of sealant.

We prefer to use a clear silicon sealer as it is easier to work with and easy to wipe the excess off. However, if you have not painted the panel, then it needs thorough cleaning with a solvent before painting or the paintwork will have a "fish eye" finish.

Drill through the base of the runner, carefully through the aluminium packing strip and into the door top. Screw the strip down with small countersunk self tapping screws. Wipe off any excess sealer. Repeat this up the rear side of the frame.

It is easier to have a dry run with the top runner i.e. drill the holes and put the strip to one side while the non-sliding glass is bedded in sealant and the aluminium glazing bar fixed on. The sliding glass may be now fitted and the top runner screwed on in its previously drilled holes. Rivet the sealing strip in place.

Offer the window lock into place but before fitting in pour some waxoyl or similar rust preventive into the box section and slosh it about to coat the inside of the frame.

Refit to the vehicle and gently close the door. The frame may need gently pulling in or out to get a satisfactory, i.e. watertight, seal against the windscreen frame. A much improved vehicle now results.

If at any stage you are not sure of the method of assembly of the top use the other side for reference. It is also sometimes a good idea to buy a scrap door top for a few pence from a Land Rover breaker to utilise the glass etc. without having to remove the top from your own vehicle. This allows you to rebuild the top without the pressure of getting the vehicle back on the road.

As the glass and glazing strips are not handed it doesn't matter which side you choose.

The take off top can then be used to remake the opposite side on your vehicle if needed.

Whilst doing the tops it is also worth replacing the door rubbers. There are three ways of doing this: Replace them with individually cut pieces as necessary, renew with a continuous strip cut to length or, by carefully cutting the edge of the flange off with a small grinder, the 90/110 type will push over the edge and give the best seal possible.

Stateside Beat

Jim Allen

The front of the engine with the timing cover off. Now is a good time to look at your timing components

Make it easier for next time

THE FRONT crankshaft seal is leaking again and you're left with two choices. Either ignore the growing oil slick in your driveway or go through the onerous process of pulling the timing cover to replace the seal.

Early Land Rover engineers must have figured that the seals were forever because they hid them behind a riveted-on mud shield. The seal can be reached only by removing the timing cover and prying the seal out from the backside.

Well, there's no getting around having to pull the cover this time, but make it easy on yourself for next time (yes, rest assured, there will be a next time) by making the seal easily accessible from the outside.

Step by step

Here is a step by step process for modifying the cover so the mud shield is removable for seal replacement at a later date.

Step 1 - Drain the cooling system and remove the fan, water pump pulley, fan shroud, radiator and overflow tank.

Step 2 - Remove the front crankshaft pulley by first bending back the locking tabs to gain access to the combination bolt/hand-crank dog. With the trans in gear and the handbrake applied, the nut can usually be broken loose by hand. If not, here are two methods for removing it.

Method 1: With a 1-7/16 socket, long extension and air impact wrench, reach through the front PTO hole and "zap" the bolt loose.

Method 2: With a 1-7/16 socket and long breaker bar, position the socket on the pulley bolt with the breaker bar against the chassis on the right side frame rail. With ignition coil wire disconnected, crank engine briefly with the starter. Keep everyone's hands well clear during this operation.

The drive pulley comes off next. It slides forward off the crankshaft snout. Seven times out of ten, it will slide off with little or no effort. During those other times, the use of applied force comes into play. A three-jawed puller will do the trick or a prybar used between the pulley and the timing cover.

Once the pulley is off, look at the sealing surface on the pulley for signs of grooving. If the sealing surface is anything more than very slightly grooved, the pulley will need replacement. An inexpensive method of repairing grooved pullies is to install a "speedy sleeve". This is a very thin sleeve that is installed over the existing sealing surface and once installed, it gives the new seal a fresh surface to work on. It has the added benefit of slightly increasing the diameter of the pulley and the seal ends up fitting a bit tighter.

Step 3 - Remove the front cover. There aren't any real tricky parts here, but save

Δ *Once drilled to 1/4", the holes are tapped for a 4mm x 70 bolt. Alternately, once the old rivets are drilled and knocked out, self tapping screws can be installed*

Δ *The mud shield being drilled oversize to accept the 4mm bolt*

The mud shield being installed. Coat the backside of the shield with silicone sealer or Hylomar, and install the bolts ∇ *using thread sealer*

yourself some hassle by marking the location of the various types and lengths of bolts. Also, make note of the bolts that project into the water jacket so that you can seal the threads of those bolts at reassembly time using teflon thread sealer. When the cover is off, scrape all old gasket material from the face of the block taking care not to contaminate the chain mechanism with scrapings.

Step 4 - With the cover outer face up on a workbench, drill out the 8 rivets with a 9/64 inch drill bit. The shanks of the long rivets can be driven out with a small punch.

Step 5 - Drill the holes once again with a 1/8 inch drill.

Step 6 - With a 4mm x 0.70 tap, or similar non-metric size, thread the holes all the way through.

An alternate method is to use self-tapping screws, though drilling and tapping is the neatest job.

Step 7 - Drill the holes in the mudshield to 9/64 inch.

Step 8 - Knock out the old seal and thoroughly clean the cover and mud shield in spirits or petrol.

Step 9 - Install the new seal flush with the cover. The garter spring and lip face inwards.

Step 10 - Smear a light coating of silicone sealer on the back side of the mud shield and install it. Seal the threads of the bolts with Teflon thread sealer to prevent leaks.

Step 11 - Reinstall the timing cover after smearing a light film of silicone sealer on each gasket face and sticking the gaskets onto the block. Remember to seal the bolts that project into the water jacket with thread sealer.

The area where the oil sump mates to the cover will need a thicker coating of sealer, especially if the sump gasket took a beating. If the sump gasket is very badly torn, a replacement is best fitted.

Step 12 - Reinstall the pulley, making sure that the seal race is clean and lubricated with motor oil or petroleum jelly. Torque the nut to 150 foot pounds and re-engage the lock tabs.

Step 13 - Reinstall the water pump pulley, fan, belt, shroud, radiator, etc., and refill the cooling system.

Step 14 - As contamination of the motor oil with coolant and debris has likely resulted, it's best to drain it and replace it with fresh oil.

Step 15 - Start the engine and check for oil and coolant leaks. Be sure to recheck coolant levels once the thermostat has opened.

Yes, this was a somewhat onerous job! Still, take heart, the next time it will be less than a one hour job with only the pulley itself needing removal to gain access to the mud shield and seal.

The basics

By Geoff McAuley

WITH EVER increasing garage costs, and a proliferation of cheap equipment currently available, many owners are turning their thoughts to performing their own welding tasks. So what is available to the home enthusiast, and which is the best choice.

SIP Weldmate 140 Arc Welder ▷

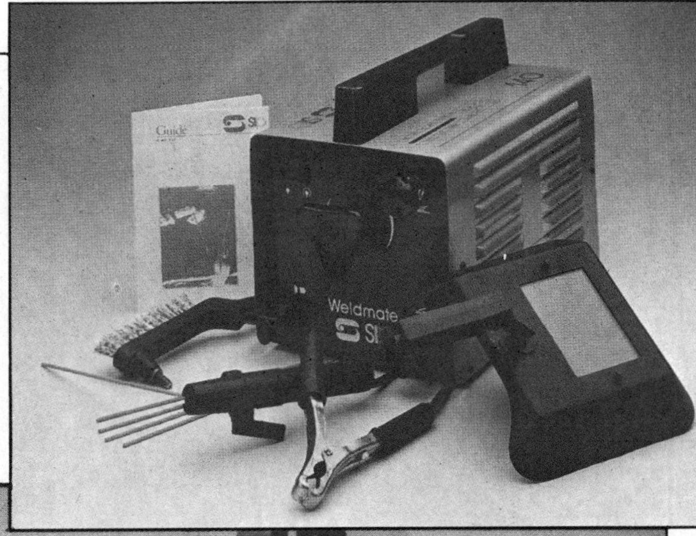

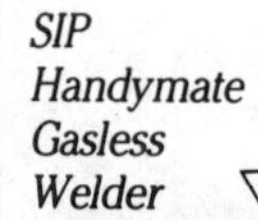

SIP Handymate Gasless Welder ▽

THERE ARE currently four main welding processes open to the amateur:

1 OXY ACETYLENE GAS
2 MANUAL METAL ARC (MMA)
3 METAL INERT GAS (MIG)
4 TUNGSTEN INERT GAS (TIG)

With all these systems, the basic principle of welding is the same, i.e. the structure of the pieces of metal to be welded, (colloquially called "the job"), is heated until molten, at which point the molecules can flow together. Often an amount of filler material is added by melting into the weld a rod or wire of the same material as the job.

Although the basic principles are the same, there are important differences in the equipment and techniques, so we'll discuss the pros and cons of each method.

Oxy Acetylene

As the name suggests, the heat required to form the weld is produced by burning the gas acetylene, in oxygen. Both gases are stored in high pressure cylinders, the acetylene in dissolved form at around 225 lb/square inch, and the oxygen at a much higher 2,500 lb/square inch.

Since the welding process needs only a few lb/square inch, regulators need to be fitted at the bottle necks. These regulators are adjustable, and usually have a dial to indicate the chosen pressure. A second guage is used on each cylinder to indicate the pre-regulator pressure, which tells the operator how much gas remains.

By turning on valves at the cylinder necks, the gases are allowed to flow along special rubber hoses, (red for acetylene, blue for oxygen), to a torch which has a mixing chamber in its hand grip. Two further valves control the gas at the torch, before it is fed into a single narrow bore copper nozzle, screwed into the end of the torch.

Several nozzle sizes are available, and a number stamped on the side indicates the size of the orifice. Number 1 is the smallest, this being suitable for thin sheet welding jobs. Most home users will require only perhaps five nozzles, in the size range 1 to 10.

Method of use

Having inserted the nozzle appropriate to the job, and checked that the torch valves are closed, the gas supply pressure is set by opening the cylinder valves and noting the output pressure indication. A good starting point is 3 lb/square inch for the oxygen, 6 lb/square inch for the acetylene.

With goggles fitted, turn on the acetylene valve at the torch, and ignite. Increase the valve opening until the flame roars, then reduce it until the roar ceases, and a black sooty plume appears at the end of the flame. Now slowly open the torch oxygen valve until a slightly rounded intense blue flame appears in the centre of an orange flame.

If the blue flame is small and sharply pointed, the oxygen flow should be reduced, if the flame is poorly defined and "yellowy", more oxygen is required. The tip of this blue centre is the hottest part of the flame, and is thus the area which is used for melting "the job".

It's best to practice on a few scraps of sheet steel by creating a molten pool, and then slowly running the torch along the test piece, melting the metal as you go. Small circular motions with the torch will help to control the heat, and it will soon become clear that dwelling in one place for too long will burn a hole right through the metal.

When the procedure of controlled melting has been mastered, a welding rod can be introduced into the flame. Slight dabbing movements will drop blobs of molten rod into the pool.

The final stage is to join together two test pieces, with and without the filler rod. it will be seen that the heat of the weld causes the metal to distort, and this is something that will have to be taken into account when welding for real. Often, firm clamping of the metal components will reduce the effects of distortion, but successful welding of thin panels with oxy acetylene takes a high level of competence.

Manual Metal Arc

This system is commonly known as "stick welding", because the filler rod, which is manufactured from the same material as "the job", is rather like a short stick. One end is fastened into a gun like holder, to which is connected an electrical cable. Another cable is attached by means of a Bulldog clip to the job, and a voltage is delivered across these cables.

The welder itself is essentially a "controllable step down transformer". That is to say it reduces the 240 volt mains supply to around 20 volts, but increases the available current from 13 amp to, typically, 120 amp. When the welding electrode makes contact with the job, a high current flows which melts both the rod and the job. An effect known as arcing occurs at the tip of the rod, and this encourages molten metal to be transfered from the rod to the job.

To avoid contamination of the weld due to oxidation, a substance known as flux is used. This is usually present in the form of a coating encrusted around the rod which melts as the weld is created. The flux

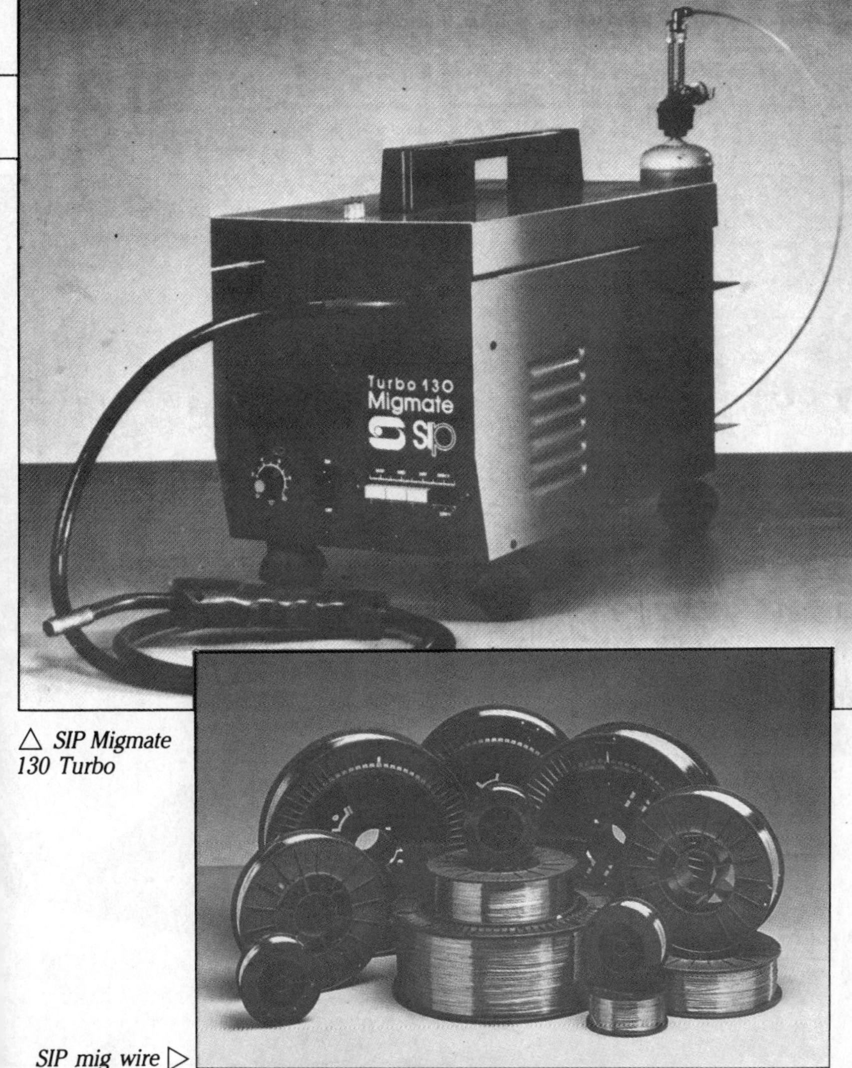

△ *SIP Migmate 130 Turbo*

SIP mig wire ▷

# of welding

forms a coating of slag on the weld which can be tapped away with a small hammer when cool.

Method of Use

In order to permit sufficient current to flow, it's important to ensure that the area to be welded is clean. Similarly, the Bulldog clip must be connected to a clean area of metal. The current output on the machine is set according to the thickness of the metal to be welded, and the end of the rod is tapped against the job.

Once the arc is "struck", the rod is moved along the path of the intended weld, and the hand is gradually lowered towards the job as the rod is consumed. It's important to store the rods in a dry location, because a damp flux can impair the ability to strike an arc.

Safety measures include the wearing of gauntlets and suitably durable clothing. It's also vitally important to use an appropriate face mask with a British Standards specification anti-glare screen. Similar eye protection must be worn by anyone else observing the welding operation, otherwise serious eye damage can occur.

Metal Inert Gas (MIG)

In recent years small MIG outfits have become increasingly popular as prices have fallen. In many ways the welding process is similar to the MMA system, but in the case of a MIG, the welding filler comes in the form of a reel of wire which is automatically fed through the nozzle of a gun as the trigger is depressed.

The flux coating is replaced with a shrouding gas which is stored in a pressurised cylinder, and which is fed automatically from the gun nozzle along with the filler wire. The type of gas is chosen to suit the material being welded. The net effect of this is to provide a weld of high quality with a minimum of expertise from the operator.

MIG is suitable for aluminium or steel welding, and the welding wire has to be of course, of the same material as the job.

It is possible to get a MIG setup without the need for a gas bottle. This is the gasless type, the shrouding gas being formed by a special flux-impregnated wire. Gasless MIGs are particularly useful for operating in windy condition, where conventional shrouding gas might be blown away from the area of the weld. They are also rather cheaper to buy than a gas model, but the finished weld rather lacks the quality appearance of that produced with a gas type MIG.

Method of Use

There are three settings to consider on a MIG welder.

1. The gas pressure, which is usually judged by turning the regulator knob by a predetermined amount.
2. The output current, this having a similar effect to MMA welding, i.e. the thicker the metal to be welded, the higher the current requirement.
3. The wire feed speed. This is automatically governed by the current setting, but some fine adjustment is possible with an additional control knob on the machine front panel.

Thankfully the manufacturer usually provides comprehensive guidelines in the instruction manual to set the beginner on the right tracks. Safety precautions are very much the same as for MMA welding.

Tungsten Inert Gas (TIG)

This is rather specialised equipment in which the MMA welding electrode is replaced with a tungsten spike. Once the arc is struck between the electrode and the job, an intense flame appears into which can be fed a filler rod, (rather like oxy acetylene).

Because of the hardness and high melting temperature of the tungsten electrode, it doesn't melt like a mild steel rod would. TIG machines can provide superb quality welds, particularly in metals like stainless steel, but prices usually start at around £1,000. The company Cebora markets a "Pocket Pulse TIG 100" for about £300, and although this is a fine little machine, it has only an alternating current output, and cannot therefore be used for welding aluminium.

Brazing

Rather like soldering, the brazing process entails heating the job to a sufficiently high temperature to permit a molten filler rod to fuse onto the surface. The job itself is not melted, and so the temperatures involved are lower than those present during welding.

Brazed joints aren't as strong as welded ones, so should not be used for structurally important jobs such as chassis repairs. Both oxy acetylene and TIG can be used as a heat source for brazing, but an MMA outfit will require an additional piece of equipment called a carbon arc torch. This device produces a flame by creating an arc between a pair of carbon electrodes.

Spot Welding

Spot welding involves squeezing two sheets of metal between special tongs, then passing a high current through them. The electrical resistance of the job creates sufficient localised heat to weld the sheets together.

Purpose built spot welders are probably of limited use to the home user, but low cost add-on devices can be bought which attach to an MMA machine. As with all electric welding processes, the job has to be thoroughly cleaned beforehand.

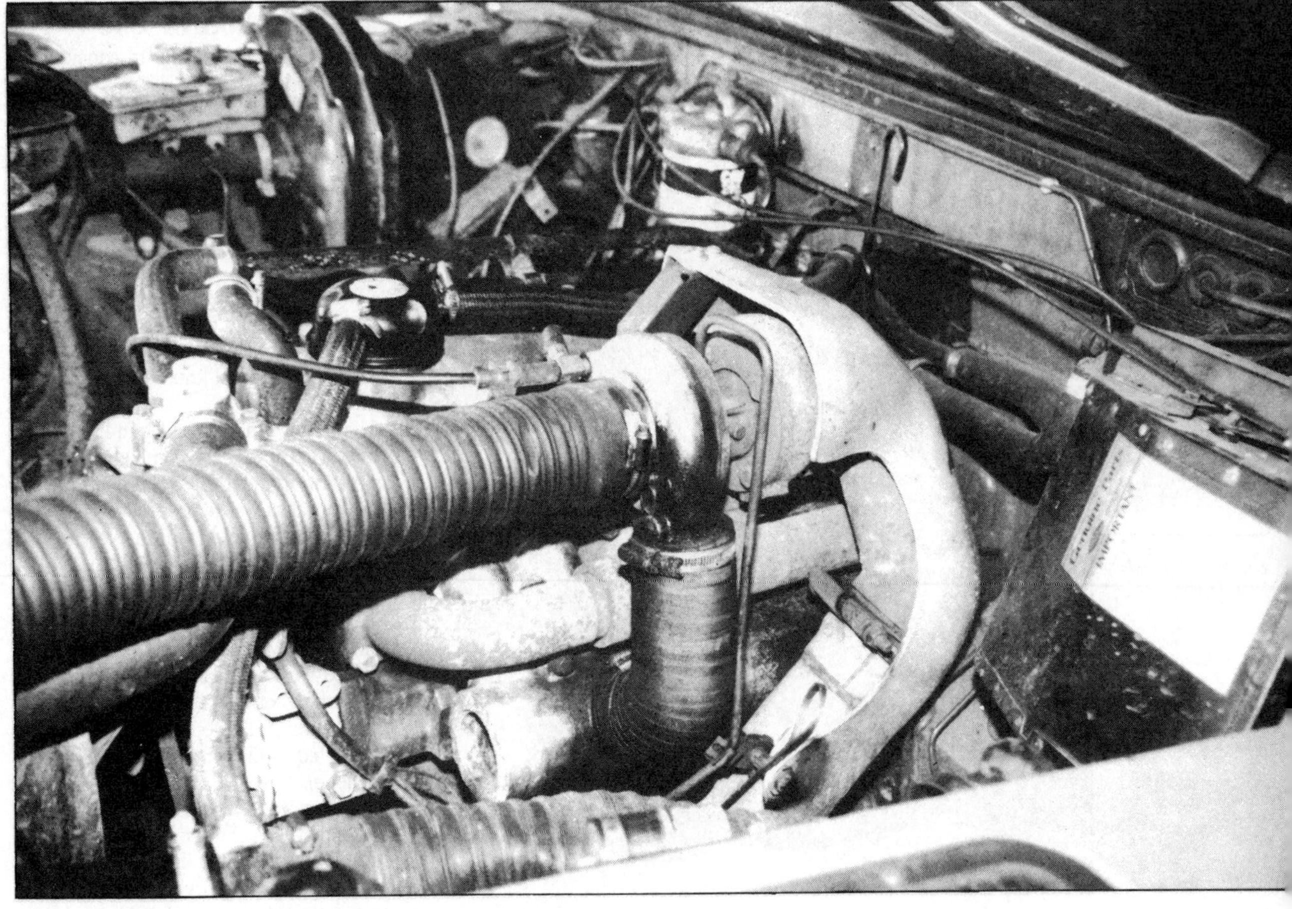

BUYING A NINETY

Used Ninetys —

Buying any used Land Rover can be worrying, but the high prices asked for Ninetys tend to compound problems for fearful purchasers. We examine the Ninety used market and show you what to look for.

THE NINETY, like any Land Rover, is essentially a working vehicle and prone to abuse in the hands of uncaring owners. Conversely, many Ninetys do seem to be lovingly looked after, right to the point when they are sold off to make way for the next.

Yet most fall somewhere between these two categories, making it difficult for the would-be buyer to assess a vehicle's true condition — pristine bodywork doesn't guarantee mechanical condition and vice-versa.

Thankfully, Ninetys are still relatively new on the market, so the chances of finding one bodged together using all manner of secondhand and non-genuine parts is rare. So, too, are high mileages.

But it is vitally important to have a good idea of the known trouble spots in the Ninety design and use this knowledge to build a realistic picture of the vehicle's overall health. This is where this second-hand buying guide will be useful.

To make matters simple, we've split this article into the various drivetrain and body/chassis areas, looking subjectively at each. With commonsense and keen eyesight, you should be able to put together the 'health' jigsaw on every Ninety you come across.

What we haven't done is labour the 'what to look for' points that apply to any used vehicle, whether Land Rover or commonplace saloon. The Ninety has a large number of unique troublespots that spoil what is otherwise a sound vehicle. Spotting these is half the battle!

Models and Variants

Since any Land Rover is like a glorified Meccano set, it is possible to build a 'bitsa' Ninety from a pile of dissembled donor vehicles or parts. In such cases, (although it is unlikely that this is widespread practice yet), the prefix on the number plate might bear no relation to the actual age or specification of the vehicle.

To bypass this hazard, there are detail changes that have been made to the Ninety that will help you place it in an approximate year of manufacture to check whether it is 'genuine' or not.

Ninetys have been offered in soft top, truck cab/tilt, hard top and station wagon form and initially retained the traditional galvanised body cappings and recessed door handles of the previous series. Bumpers too were galvanised, as were the grab handles/'casual' towing handles at the rear. The rain gutter on hard tops and truck cabs was also galvanised.

This specification lasted from the Ninety's introduction in May 1984 through to mid 1986, when body cappings were colour matched to the rest of the paintwork, new non-recessed door handles were introduced and hardtop/truck cab rain gutters were changed to an integral painted alloy construction.

Most dealers refer to this as '1987 specification' or 'black bumper', as bumpers were finished in matt black.

◀ *Turbo Diesel* ▲ *V8*

shop carefully

While the hardtop and truck cab variants have stayed the course, the soft top version more or less died out in 1986/1987. Even then it was rarely ordered by dealers and retained for the Armed Forces.

With some ex-military vehicles now being released onto the market, it's important to note that these versions also had the early One-Ten split construction doors with sliding windows — these were *never* a civilian market option.

Doors are a good guide to vehicle age. Civilian market door types were restricted to one piece wind-up window designs. 'Stick' type internal door lock operators and one-piece trim was used for pre-mid 1986 'galvanised' capping vehicles and a more modern trim with recessed internal door lock operators for doors fitted to '1987 specification' vehicles. The latter also lost the external recessed door handle to a plastic non-recessed push button type.

Just to confuse matters, in early 1986, there was a very brief run of Ninetys with recessed door handles, early door trim *and* colour coded body cappings (minus the pre 1987 specification 'dummy' galvanised trim on the door). This heralded the factory's change to 1987 specification and even the Australian Camel Trophy Ninetys were to this oddball spec.

These are the major visible changes that many dealers use to check age against registration number. Seating is not such a good guide, with only the LWB Series 3 plain squabs and frames being discontinued around mid 1986 as an option to go on. Dashboards, instruments and body panels have remained largely the same.

Obviously engine type is the other guide to age. Ninetys from the 1984 launch to May 1985 were fitted with just the 2.25 litre four cylinder petrol engine or 2.5 litre diesel, both linked to 5 speed gearboxes. In August 1985, the four cylinder petrol engine was upgraded to 2.5 litres, but May of that year saw the 114bhp V8 version of the Ninety launched. It wasn't until October 1986 that the 134bhp V8 and the diesel turbo became available and the naturally aspirated diesel was sidelined for the export market.

If you are in the market for a V8 version, it is imperative that you find one that was factory built. The LT85 five speed gearbox and four pinion rear axle used for this model are both essential to cope with the power, although V8's can be fitted to all other Ninety gearboxes, but with predictable results. Check the logbook!

Again these are broad areas of definition for model and year and there will be tales of factory built V8 soft tops with 1987 specification doors and so on. Largely though, these will be rare factory development vehicles released into the dealer network and not around in great enough numbers to worry the average buyer.

Body and chassis

Having matched specification against logbook and registration prefix, take a good look at the body and chassis. Most Ninetys will have a few marks or dents, but check for scuffed floor panels, almost paintless and polished rear load areas and the inevitable straw in nooks and crannies. This is the golden rule that never really fails to separate farm vehicles from private owner machines.

▶

Check interiors for tell-tale signs of hard use

Vinyl trimmed seats and centre cubby box all in reasonably good condition.

A right-old mixture of seats. this particular vehicle has had a hard l

A farm vehicle will also usually be a diesel or turbo diesel (sounds trite, but its normally the case); private owner a petrol four cylinder, higher specification turbo diesel or V8.

Check for paint overspray, especially around the sills, fuel tank, door rubbers and lower seat belt mountings on the seat box. No-one, least of all the trade, masks Land Rovers properly when refinishing paintwork — these items always show the evidence of any respraying. Farmers and commercial users will rarely bother to correct body faults prior to selling on; private buyers might in the hope of increasing value marginally.

If you can accept a few dents, then there should be little problem. But bear in mind that body sides are expensive and difficult to replace and the one piece doors are also horrendously expensive to buy — you can't reskin them.

Whatever your personal views on what is acceptable and what isn't in terms of body condition, try to assess how the vehicle got its battle scars. A shallow depression in a side panel that shows the flange of the wheelbox as a crease might have been caused on a farm by a cow leaning on it (the most common form of damage to farm vehicles), but myriad small gouges and dings usually mean its been carelessly off-roaded. Time to look at the chassis!

Basically, heavy off-roading leaves its mark underneath. The gearbox crossmember (rectangular section till mid 1986; tubular after that) is made from steel as thick as tissue paper and dents easily. So too does the tubular steering guard fitted as part of the 1987 specification. Check them for damage.

Also take a good look at the rear trailing arm forward mounts — are they slightly dog-eared? — and the face of the front axle differential case. All these suffer quickly and are usually too costly to remedy at the time of sale.

All these points will help you build the picture, but don't worry about finding structural rust. Being cathode dipped, the chassis is well protected by paint, although crash damage might change matters slightly. Look for evidence of welding or creasing if you feel that all is not right.

Suspension

Ninetys, because they are soft riding across country, tend to be driven too quickly in the rough and suffer from suspension wear. This is normally restricted to the rubber bushes used to give compliance and re-bushing is simple and relatively cheap.

Bush wear shows up as a series of thumps and bangs when on and off power and when the axles move over the road or track surface. It is easy to isolate it to front or rear, but don't confuse it with worn shock absorbers or their bushes — it's a much deeper frequency thump from the suspect corner when that happens.

Farm vehicles suffer from worn sus-

County-trim seats, recessed door trim and new-style door lock.

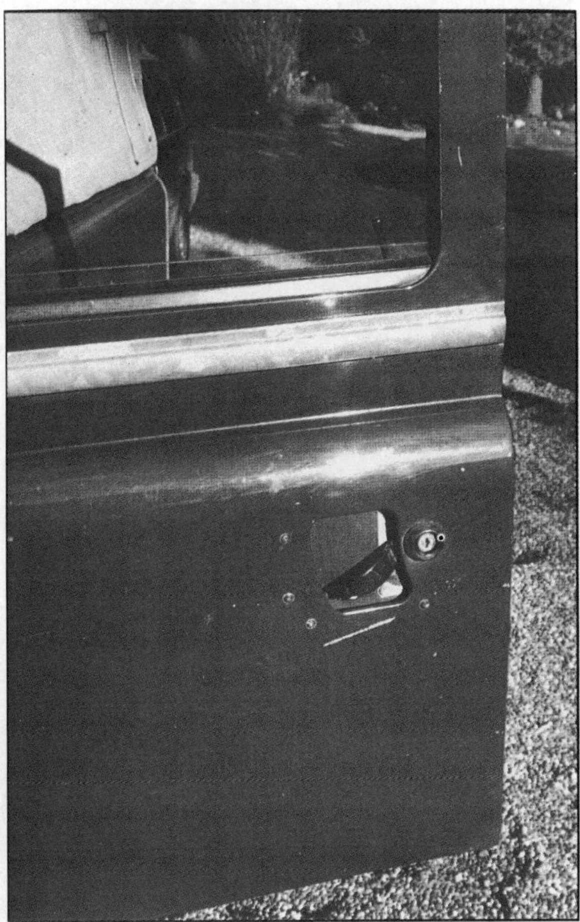

Series III style recessed door handles, protruding push/pull door lock, galvanised door capping.

pension far more than road only Ninetys. But heavily off-roaded Ninetys are usually the worst culprits and poor suspension condition will usually be linked to equally poor body and chassis condition. Most owners who use their Ninetys for recreational off-roading reckon to need a total rebush every 10,000 miles.

If a Ninety has been pushed to the limit off-road, especially when loaded, it is common for the top eye of the rear shock absorbers to be ripped off. This is because Ninety shock absorbers normally act in the same way as axle straps. Check for evidence of re-welding or fractures — if you find them, repeat your examination of the underside and suspension bushes.

Engines

The 2.5 litre engines, both petrol and diesel, were initially subject to a number of dealer recalls, with a batch during 1985 having escaped with non case hardened cam followers. It's unlikely that you will come across one that escaped this recall, but as a rule, the top end is always the weak link with these engines. So too is bore wear — they require regular oil changes to prolong life.

Similarly, the camshaft drive belt (which replaced the chain on the earlier series 2.25 litre engines) has been known to break prematurely, with bent pushrods and broken followers being the end result. The belt should be changed every 30,000 miles and is quoted as a principal service item — ask for proof of its change if the mileage of your selected vehicle is over the 30,000 mile mark.

It's also worth looking for oil leaks since both engines are not known for their oil-tight qualities, especially around the seal at the back of rear main bearing. To repair that means taking the engine out — a costly and major job.

The turbo diesel and the diesel both suffer from piston blow-by at low mileages and the turbo variant especially tends to blow oil via a breather into the air cleaner, prematurely clogging the expensive filter. There's no dealer cure for this, so look for excessive oil staining on the filter or oil dripping from the filter housing.

The V8 conversely is a relative paragon of reliability, easily reaching 150,000 miles without overhaul as long as it is regularly servied. The major problem area here is camshaft wear and blocked crankcase breathers. The first is easy to detect by the noise; the latter often produces clouds of exhaust smoke.

Largely, all Land Rover engines protest when in poor condition. Diesels usually won't start and get very clattery and smokey; the petrol engines rattle and smoke and the V8 will literally eat itself in a short space of time after a serious problem develops, due simply to the number of reciprocating parts. In good condition, the four cylinder units are agricultural but smooth enough; the V8 is well balanced and sweet. However, allow

Lovingly cherished, or seriously abused?

Above left: Interior paintwork scratched away to bare metal in the driver's footwell.

Above: An item that will obviously need replacing.

Left: How many times has the driver scrambled into and out of this Ninety?

for lack of servicing and check the usual items such as oil colour, filters and so on.

Radiators fail habitually. Look for signs of leakage or let the vehicle stand and tick-over for a while to check for temperature fluctuation. In good condition, a Ninety's temperature gauge will read dead on halfway, even when worked hard.

Gearboxes, tranfer box and axles

Apart from gearbox/transfer box unreliability caused by excessive abuse or mismatching a four cylinder gearbox to a V8 engine, most Ninetys have a major problem with their transmission.

This is the transfer box knocking itself out of low ratio into neutral during harsh 'power on, power off' tactics. Nearly all Ninetys suffer from this to differing degrees, and it's not confined to any particular engine or model. If you can be brutal enough without incurring the wrath of the seller, you can check the severity of the problem, but don't overdo it to the point of doing any damage. Towing a loaded trailer usually provides a suitable load to invoke the problem. Strangely, the One-Ten does not display this awkward habit.

Overall though, Ninety gearboxes are tough. They might whine at high mileages and be stiff when cold, but they rarely jump out of gear on the overrun or fail altogether. Confine your tests to synchromesh and general performance and use your ears to tell you what condition the box is generally in.

Axles on the other hand can pose numerous problems. Differential failure, especially at the front, is usually the result of hard off-road use, although the rear unit can whine badly prior to failure if the vehicle has been habitually overloaded or waded without the oil being checked for water contamination. Halfshaft failure is rare.

It's also worth listening for clunks, whines and squeaks from the rear propshaft front joint. These are regular offenders and should one fail, a flapping propshaft can do all manner of damage to itself, the exhaust system and underside.

Brakes and steering

The Ninety braking system is generally excellent with the disc/drum combination well up to stopping the vehicle, even in loaded V8 form. The Range Rover disc warping habit hasn't been carried over to the Ninety, despite the similarity of fittings, but it's worth checking for scored discs and worn drums. Have a good look at the brake pipes for damage, especially on the rear axle where they can get snagged.

The steering is reliable at moderate mileages, although the power steering pump can leak at the pulley as the bearings wear. Check this visibly and even pull on the pulley to check whether the bearings will allow it to move forward noticeably.

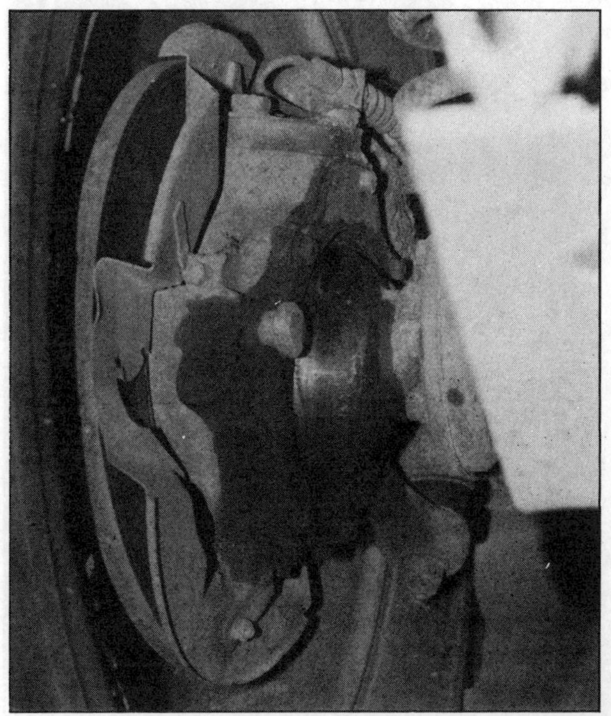

Above right: Interior trim that has been half kicked to death should tell you something about the care and attention that the owner has lavished on the rest of the vehicle.

Above: Oil leaks will inevitably lead to expense on repairs.

Right: Not a structural fault, it's true, but it makes for an untidy vehicle.

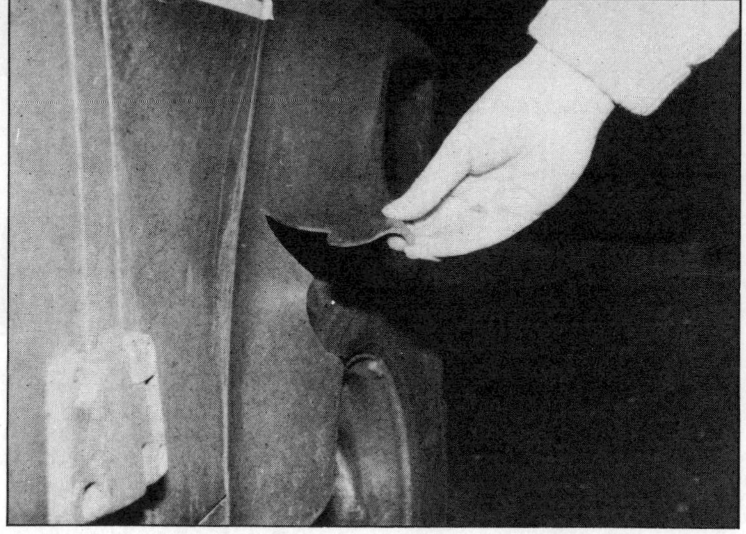

Without power assistance, the steering is heavy and feels entirely different — PAS is a definite boon.

Obviously, the Ninety will suffer from ball joint wear, but more important is the condition of the drag links around the front axle. The linkage set-up from hubs to the steering drop arm is complicated and easily damaged off-road. If the main drag link between the hubs is bent, have it replaced. This is because, once deformed (and it's very easy to do), secondary oscillation sets in when the vehicle is driven. This will quickly fracture it, leaving you with no steering control whatsoever!

Cursory examination of the swivel hub faces and seals should be included in your list of points to look at.

Accessories

Almost every Ninety seems to have some form of accessory or non-standard part fitted to it and it's as well to know whether they are worth the extra money you might have to pay for them.

Winches are a regular fitment, but for self-recovery, only 8000lb models are worth considering. Electric front mount winches should be used with a split charge system and two batteries. If just one battery is used, check its condition — it might have been fatally drained at some stage. PTO winches are expensive to repair and offer generally less useful pulling rates.

All manner of tyres can be fitted, ranging from 205 section radials to 750 size crossplies. Crossplies are not speed rated for V8s and regardless of Ninety model must not rub on the chassis (the steering stops are adjustable for this) — it's an MOT fail if they do. 750's are also too big for Range Rover RoStyle rims — One-Ten rims only should be used.

Bullbars are of debatable worth and a matter of personal taste, but roofracks must be fitted with additional front and rear tiebars if fitted to 1987 specification vehicles — the alloy roof guttering will not support them, when loaded, alone.

Of course, some vehicles may be fully Safari equipped and some 'as they left the factory' — again it depends what you want — but do check that if rear seats and side windows have been retrofitted to commercial vehicles (subject to VAT), the tax has been paid. You could inherit a lot of Customs and Excise trouble if you don't.

That more or less concludes the major points on Ninety trouble areas. Of course, there are some 'Friday afternoon' vehicles around, which cause untold trouble and others are 100 per cent reliable — one can't be too careful or thorough when checking them over.

But generally, most Ninety owners tend to feel they have bought well and a good vehicle at a good price has got to be a bargain in anyone's book.

Happy hunting!

△ *The Lightweight — first choice for UK off-roading.*

Choosing your

WHAT MAKES a good off-roader? How much preparation does your vehicle really need? How do you cope with the unexpected? These, and thousands of other questions, are often asked by novice and experienced off-roaders alike. Tim Webster delves into his off-roading past to find the simple answers.

BY AND large, off-roading is like any other sport, pastime, hobby — call it what you will. And that's because it is far from being an exact science.

Indeed, ask a typically simple question — such as 'Which tyre do I use?' — of the 'experts' who seem to form the off-road 'Establishment', and you'll more than likely get a series of quite different answers. Sorting out who's right, and who's wrong can then take an age, assuming you are prepared to experiment with your vehicle, your money… and, quite possibly, your life.

Unfortunately, most newcomers to off roading are reluctant to experiment with different equipment, techniques or even tyres. Instead, they assume all Land Rovers are equal, get locked into the off-roader image, and spend their money on bullbars and other quite useless vehicle accessories that do nothing to improve off-road performance.

Then they find out just how much local farmers charge to rescue them from the clutches of bottomless bogs.

I suppose that, over the eight or nine years I've been off-roading regularly, I've seen it all. Owners of brand new Range Rovers, ready to weep because they've dinged a previously unblemished panel; hardened overlanders sinking into the track they're driving because they're carrying two tons of recovery gear; enthusiasts sweating over repaying a £5,000 bank loan, taken out just to *equip* their aging — and unreliable — 110 with off-road equipment.

And, to my mind, the worst sort — the ones who insist on tackling difficult routes on nothing better than road-treaded 205 radials, just because the tyres allow them to do upwards of 90mph on the tarmac sections in between off-road tracks. And anyway, they claim they don't go off-roading that often, so why fit off-road tyres.

I include these examples to prove one particular point. Successful off-roading calls for a sensible approach, and, where possible, a dedicated choice of the right vehicle. One that is sensibly and *logically* equipped, not over-burdened. And one that gives you self-sufficiency, whether you're with a party of other off-roaders, or going it alone.

That sensible approach means that off-roading *can* be made simple. And it needn't cost the earth either (although it often does). This is the theme I'm taking with these articles, and I'll be drawing not only on my own experience — and, boy, have I made mistakes — but others I would consider to be the 'elite' of off-roaders.

So, whether you're a hopeful novice, or have bags of experience, there should be something for you here.

Successful off-roading is largely a matter of solving a big puzzle. And that puzzle is how to make a relatively heavy vehicle pass over unmade tracks and road.

This applies to all off-roading, whether you are taking to the green roads of Wales, or the pistes of the Sahara. The first step towards a first-time solution is to work out what are the main hazards of the area where you're going to drive, and what do you want to carry — people and equipment-wise — in your vehicle.

And, most importantly, what vehicle is most suitable. This in particular is the first

△ *90 Hardtop, 2.5 diesel — safe, secure and reliable.*

off roader

△ *Rollovers can happen easily, and in the most unexpected places.*

'Question' of the series I'd like to try and answer.

Choosing the right vehicle for the sort of off-roading you want to do is a subject largely ignored by the various 'How To . . .' books on off-roading. And contrary to popular belief, not every Land Rover model is tailor-made for every type of off-roading.

For example, if you are planning to confine your off-roading to the UK (which has more than its fair share of wet moors, sodden forests, and quagmirish tracks), the emphasis has got to be on the more lightweight of the Land Rover range.

At the top of your shopping list, if you're in the market for a vehicle for UK off-roading, has got to be the S2 or S3 Lightweight. It's basic, cheap, shrugs off the inevitable body scrapes and dings, and has remarkable side-slope stability.

Behind that I'd list the Ninety (in basic hardtop form), the 88″ and various Series One short wheelbase models as having equal merit.

Venturing further afield calls for more payload capability and more room, and it's here that the 109″ One-Ten and FC101 score, with perhaps the Discovery and Range Rover completing the list for those keen on long distance touring and comfort.

Personally, I never vary from this list, and often wince if I'm accompanied by a heavy One-Ten on my frequent forays into Wales or Yorkshire. On the other hand, experience shows that a Ninety can be good on long overseas trips, but only if there are two in the vehicle, and you're used to travelling light. I wouldn't recommend varying from this formula one iota otherwise.

Why? For a start, despite what anyone says, off-roading is hard on any vehicle. The heavier it is, the harder you are asking it to work, and the more strain you are placing on its drivetrain.

A heavy vehicle, even unladen, is also more prone to bogging, and is more difficult to recover. All of a sudden, it's easy to get into a vicious circle — your vehicle bogs frequently, so you take more recovery equipment. That in turn makes it heavier, so it bogs even more, and takes more equipment to recover it.

So, for the UK at least, it makes sense to go for the vehicle that has the least weight. This is why I put the Lightweight at the top of my list.

For the novice, it's ideal, because it is cheap, rugged, durable and shrugs off body scrapes. It's also economical to repair. Yet seasoned off-roaders, many of which could no doubt afford a far more expensive Land Rover also often opt for it because they appreciate the logic of the vehicle, expecially for UK use.

The Ninety is also a popular choice for UK off-roading, but it does have a number of drawbacks. For example, in County form, it has trim that can be spoiled by muddy peat, and also the argument for a lightweight vehicle starts to be compromised.

It can also be expensive to repair, as I found to my cost when I inadvertently rolled mine. The repair bill for my Ninety was somewhere in the region of £5,000 (using new parts — secondhand can be difficult to find); a badly rolled Lightweight (or standard 88″ for that matter) can often be reassembled for less than £1000 using used parts.

Some off-roaders take a pragmatic view about cost. A good friend of mine, and one of the best off-roaders I've ever come across, runs an early Ninety. The purchase price of the vehicle four years ago was £5,000, expensive in those days for a vehicle to be used as an off-road machine. Yet he said at the time that he would never really expect to get much more for the

 ▷

△ *The One Ten, — ideal for long distances, wide open spaces and firm tracks.*

V8 90 with full tilt protected by a roll cage. ▷

vehicle on resale than the return from breaking it for parts.

And that's because, today, there isn't a straight panel left on it, and with around 150,000 miles under its belt, there aren't many people who would buy it complete. Yet the pragmatism stems from the fact that he sees that initial £5,000, and the estimated £4,000 per year it costs him to run and repair it, as good value for the sport he loves.

Another off-roader I had the pleasure of travelling with a few years back ran a 100" RR/LR hybrid — his answer to the search for the perfect vehicle for UK off-roading. He, like many others, took to off-road almost every other weekend, and once calculated that each day of those weekends cost him over £100 in eventual vehicle servicing and repairs alone.

For my own part, I've run three Ninety's (and a funny thing called a Suzuki SJ410 in my youth), and all required, over the years, countless new panels, suspension rebushings, sets of tyres, gearboxes and so on. Not that my brand of off-roading is harder than anyone else's. Its just that the further you go off-road, the harder it tends to get on the vehicle. Sooner or later, something (or a lot of 'somethings') either breaks or needs replacing.

Of course, if you refer back to my list of vehicles for different typs of off-roading, you'll now understand why you should apply the light weight regime to any decision process involving buying a Land Rover for an off-road trip. Weight (together with cost) is the great enemy of the off-roader, and even a long Saharan trip, using a long wheelbase model, is no excuse for succumbing to excess weight.

There is also something else to bear in mind. And that is the effect that often heavy off-road equipment will have on your calculations as to the best Land Rover for your brand of off-roading.

Given that Land Rovers come with all sorts of different engines, and different body formats, which should you go for? Again, years of experience and careful watching of other friends' mistakes has helped me put together what I believe to be the simple answer to these particular questions, in off-road terms certainly.

Given the choice, I'd always go for a Land Rover engine (rather than another manufacturer's engine transplanted) simply for the ability to find spare parts easily. And the one Land Rover engine I do like is the naturally aspirated 2.5 litre diesel. It's economical, has more than adequate power and torque, especially in low box, uses safe fuel, and lasts well.

Next in line is the near industructable 2.25 petrol engine. Again it has adequate power, and lasts well.

Both these engines are very reliable, as long as they are requlารly serviced, and that's important when your vehicle could be up to its axles in mud for a day or two, wading through deep rivers, traversing steep side slopes, or even being sorted after an accidental roll-over or capsize (which does happen quite often, contrary to popular belief).

The V8 is also a firm favourite with off-roaders because of its power. But I've seen too many V8 Land Rover drivers blow their diffs when using heavily treaded tyres.

In fact, economy is a problem off-road, and one Ninety V8 I ran would use a gallon of fuel just ticking over on a moor for an hour, and powering an electric winch.

And, finally, which body format? In the UK, I'd like to say go for a full canvas tilt (for an even lower centre of gravity and less spoilable bodywork), but too few off-roaders have the sense to fit rollbars or rollcages as well, So it's down to the ubiquitous hardtop, which at least has some roll-over protection, is lockable, and gives you an opportunity to fit a roofrack.

Δ *Clutch servo installed in a Ninety Turbo Diesel*

Reduced effort

FOR MANY, a Land Rover is a necessity, but the heaviness of the controls can make them hard to drive, particularly for the disabled. A bad back or leg can be a major problem when driving a Land Rover and the clutch is usually the hardest pedal to operated.

On all coil sprung vehicles, and most of the later Series IIIs, a servo is fitted to the brakes to reduce brake pedal effort. It is also possible to fit a remote type servo to the clutch.

The small type shown here has a 4:1 operating ratio, so reduces the pedal effort to a quarter of its former requirement. The turbo diesel engines seem to have the heaviest clutch and it is a well worth improvement even if you don't have a medical condition.

The servo is a common unit and is fitted to many older cars such as the Austin 1800, Hillman Hunter, Rover 2000 and so on. If sourced from one of these, a reconditioning kit should be fitted. New units are about £100.

Two adaptors from quarter inch to three sixteenths pipe are also needed. These are used on the Series III and 90/110 clutch master cylinder (part number 139082 at £4) and two copper washers to fit them. Also needed will be: a short length of quarter inch brake pipe with two male unions, a 'T' for the vacuum hose, a short length of vacuum pipe and odd bits of steel for mounting brackets.

If the servo is mounted as shown in the photograph, the original pipe to the slave cylinder may be bent round and fitted to the end of the servo with one of the adaptors. The other adaptor is used with the new metal quarter inch pipe to join the servo inlet to the clutch master cylinder outlet.

Cut the rubber vacuum pipe from the inlet manifold (petrol) or exhauster pump (diesel) and fit a 'T' piece. The 2.25 diesel Series III uses a suitable 'T' where the vacuum pipe leads off into the vacuum reservoir.

Connect up with a short length of vacuum hose and the system is ready to bleed. Fill with fluid and bleed at the slave cylinder in the normal way. If it won't bleed properly, bleed with the engine running and the servo working.

The much reduced pedal effort is well worth the time.

Auto boxes

Another way of reducing effort is to go automatic. One Tens and Ninetys can be converted relatively easily with Range Rover auto bits, especially if they are already V8.

The Series III is not so easy. The Borg Warner 65 or 66 gearbox can be fitted to a Land Rover transfer box with a conversion made by Ian Ashcroft (0582 761081). The gearbox will fit a V8 if the donor car is a V8; if a FX4R taxi bellhousing is used it will mate with the Rover diesel engine. It is not the fastest thing in the world, but if you need an automatic, then it's better than nothing.

The gearbox is three inches longer than standard. With a V8 conversion and a Ninety type front, this is no problem, but on a four cylinder the prop shafts need altering to suit and the mountings moving back.

A Jaguar XJ6 cable-operated gear shift mechanism is the easiest to site and does not suffer from ghost changes when there is a relative movement between body and transmission. The conversion with a V8 engine is best effected by mounting the engine further forward than normal and leaving the transfer box in its original place. A small amount of modification is needed to the floor and panelwork to accommodate the conversion.

For more details on auto conversions, ring Automatic Conversions on 0582 761081.

Driveable at last — but it took a long time getting there.

A familiar story?

By Owen Clutton

I FIRST set eyes on the vehicle nearly four years ago, when I was interviewed for a manager's job on a farm in Somerset, a position which I obtained. The old grey Land-Rover had been on the farm for most, if not all, of its life since its creation in 1959. It was a bit scruffy, with its tattered hood and dirt-encrusted bodywork, but it seemed to work fairly well.

After I had been in the job for a while, one of my bosses called me to task and queried the amount of money which I was spending on petrol. I told him that at 15 mpg it was hardly surprising. The Land Rover was pushed into a shed and I was given a Suzuki.

Two years later. I had moved back to Sussex, but the vehicle was still in my mind. I had always wanted one, so I drove down with a trailer, paid £180 and brought it back.

At that time, I was under the impression that it was fine apart from its clutch and head gasket. It seemed reasonable to me.

I am the world's worst mechanic. I have a basic knowledge of engines and things, but I tend to get lost once I attempt to delve into the entrails of any machine. However, my brother Jon knows about these things so he could do the difficult bits. No problem.

It did not take him long to replace some of the electrics and get the vehicle going. Apart from a few tappety valve noises, it was fine. We could even move it. When the snow came, I set off to test the engine. The clutch gave at the end of the drive, and I had to drag the vehicle back with my car. Our first major work was determined. John knew how to do it, so I abandoned my idea of using a fitter and set a weekend aside for the work.

The floor had obviously never come out before, because it took a morning to get the seat base out. We loosened all of the various things which one has to free to move the engine up and forward, until we came to the handbrake drum. It was solid.

In my year and more of Land Rover ownership, I have resorted to more in the way of bad language than I would previously have believed possible. Jon's words as he cursed the drum were amazing. Eventually it came free, and we were able to move the gearbox back.

Back-breaking

Our trusty Haynes was fairly detailed about how we should lift the box from the vehicle, which would have been fine except for one minor detail. We had no lifting gear. The trolley jack pushed it up only enough to get a few logs underneath it, but that was no good. I am used to handling heavy cows, so I volunteered to be a crane. I rolled the tilt back and out of the way, and heaved. It came up all right, and Jon was soon fiddling around inside it while I started to peel the years of red Somerset mud from the casing.

We fitted new plates and assembled all of the bits in reverse order of their removal. I jumped in, expecting to drive away. Nothing. There was no give at all on the thrust bearing shaft and we realised that we would have to do it all again. We must have set something wrong inside.

Another weekend. We took the whole thing apart again, and although it dismantled fairly easily, we were surprised to find that everything was as it should be. A few tightening adjustments, then reassembly once again. It still would not work.

'Bloody Land Rover', I roared in my frustration, using a phrase which has been repeated often. We started on the hydraulic system. The master cylinder seemed to be working, so I removed the other one. A simple job like that, according to the book, should have been one which even I could tackle. I replaced its seals, and put it back. Nothing. I tightened everything up, and tried again. Nothing. I swore some more and went off to my local Land Rover dealer, Gumtree Enterprises of Plumton. He gave me another cylinder, but for the Series 2A. It was the only one in stock. With a little manipulation, this went in. Still nothing.

I removed the master cylinder and made my way back to Plumpton. I got some more seals, and while I was there, I purchased another hood. Second hand, but at least it was all in one piece which is more than I could say for the old one. The seals went in, the whole thing was tightened up, and I tested it. It worked; all was well. I could concentrate on other repairs.

Just the beginning

Perhaps I should have done a more thorough check prior to purchase, because the clutch and gasket were only the beginning. The exhaust was gone, so I bought the new bits to replace the system. It went in fine, until I tried to connect the front pipe to the manifold. The bolts would not do up, and on inspection, it was cracked. The new one was angled differently, so I had to get another pipe. I tried to force the system together until I realised that the middle pipe was wrong too, so that had to come out.

We had so much trouble starting the vehicle. I have been through two dynmos, burning out the first before I found that the voltage regulator was knackered. The starter motor was no good, so that came out. We replaced the coil, HT leads and plugs, then finally the whole distributor section. I sprayed WD 40 into the starter to free it; it smoked furiously for a while and did not work again. That had to be changed. The car battery which I had found in a scrapyard failed, and I had to buy a new heavy duty one.

We had just about got the starting system to work, when I decided to get the polarity changed to fit a radio. I had already been advised on how to fit one without changing the polarity; I burned out a car radio by doing that the wrong way. The people who changed the polarity failed to earth the engine properly. When Gumtree towed the vehicle away, it was a bit embarrassing when they told me that all I had needed to do was fit a proper earth strap.

Eventually we got the vehicle to its MOT test. It passed on most things except for the brakes. We replaced pipes and cylinders and bled the system a few times until it worked. The Land Rover was finally on the road.

On the road

There's none such fools as them who think they've got it right. Within a week of the MOT, my brother was on the phone. 'It's broken down,' he said. I drove out in the car and found him blocking a busy garage forecourt. The pin securing the clutch operating shaft and sleeve had sheared, but we could not do the work there, so I bought a tow rope. I felt a bloody fool dragging the Land Rover home behind a heavily-smoking Renault. We replaced the pin with a temporary substitute which worked very well: a six inch nail, cut down for length.

With the onset of summer, improvements (sounds so much better than repairs) were restricted to minor items, such as replacing the radiator, various lights, wires, wipers and, eventually, the head gasket.

The obvious work which one does to a vehicle like this are easy to spot. What makes it more difficult is trying to anticipate what is likely to go next.

I had been out tree cutting after the hurricane last year, carrying logs across fields and bogs with the vehicle. There was a slight rattling underneath which I ignored, until I was driving home. Suddenly, while descending a hill, there was an almightly crashing from below.

I pulled over onto the verge, using only momentum to leave the road as the drive would not respond. It was dark, and my dog was going frantic inside with the noise. Fortunately, I had a torch with me and I crawled under the back, trying to ignore the heavy lorries which were pounding past. The rear diff shaft had sheared, and the drive was slamming around aimlessly. I used the tow rope and tied it up to the chassis. We drove the last few miles home at a snail's pace, using the front wheels for propulsion and in low ratio. There was a tailback of traffic all the way, and I had to stop frequently to tie the rope more securely.

When I got home, I had another look. 'That's it', I exclaimed. 'I'm going to sell it.' My brother came home later and examined it for himself. 'You need another diff.'

Constant threat

During my eighteen months of Land Rover ownership, my constant threat has been to sell the damn thing. It's a sort of ultimatum in my love-hate relationship with the beast. It comes after kicking the wheels and before relenting and going out to get whatever is needed.

Once the new diff was fitted, I thought that all would be well thereafter. I had been ignoring the increasing failure of my new clutch for ages; eventually it could no longer be treated that way and the vehicle had to be dragged to a fitter. He took the clutch apart, re-adjusted it and it worked. For a while. Then it didn't. I took it back. Now it has an extra length welded to the slave cylinder pushrod and is usuall fine. I am learning the art of double-de-clutching on first and second gears.

The carburettor was always a problem; I am told that those old ones tend to be. When it got to the stage of spraying petrol across the hot manifold, I had to do something about it. The current one had been on a fitter's shelf for years, but now works a treat. I am sure that the fuel consumption has fallen. It took three visits to another fitter before we got the timing sorted out; apparently I was using the wrong grade of petrol.

I was never terribly happy with the cosmetic side of things. There was too much grey. I bought some paint, and we started to brush-paint it. My first mishap was when a full tin of blue paint slipped out of my hand and spilled down my front. Fortunately my jeans were also blue, but now they are bluer. My brown leather shoes also sport blue streaks now, and my legs were very cosmopolitan until I managed to get the damn stuff off.

The gleaming newish white wheels contrast effectively with the smart paintwork, and generally I am pleased. My seat is called 'deluxe' (not my personal one), while the passengers face a hard cushion instead of the former wet springs. I had to swap the coat hanger for a real exhaust strap for the MOT. The windscreen washer failed in the ten minutes between fitting it and driving to the garage, but they didn't notice the nail. They did notice the failure of the rear nearside brakes, soaked as they were in oil from a weak hub seal, and these were replaced.

For sale?

Does anybody want to buy a Land Rover? The clutch might need some more work and, yes, you will have to fit a strap to hold it in reverse. But it's not much for its age, is it? How many of those pristine Japanese vehicles will still be on the road in 2018? In the meantime, as 282 EYC chases me into our fourth decade, could someone lend me one of those stickers? You know the one, 'I hate my Land Rover'. That's for the bad days.

But those are forgotten today. The sun is shining, the roof is off and I'm going for a drive. I've got my brand new Wombles tape to play, and if they won't let me play it at home, I'll play it to everyone in the street. At least it will give them a laugh.

Mechanical dabbling may not be quite my scene, but at least I have something to show now for all the disasters along the way. If anybody is contemplating renovating a Land Rover, I wish them the very best. I can't believe that anyone could have as much trouble as I did, but maybe these notes will give some guidance as to what can go wrong.

Okay, I relent. I'll have a 'Luv my Larry Landie' sticker after all. Perhaps, when all is said and done, well perhaps I do. Just a bit.

And if you *do* want to buy it, it'll cost you!

Owen Clutton with the Rover he loves to hate.

Stuck in the mud?

DURING the last five years, David Bowyer, who runs the Overlander Off Road Driving Centre, has developed, tested and manufactured two new ground anchor accessories. Ground anchors are essential items of equipment for all serious off roaders who have winches fitted to their vehicles.

Securing a vehicle in one spot and using its front mounted winch to recover another vehicle is always a problem. Overlander has therefore developed the 'Wedgit'. This wedge shaped wheel chock, which is placed in front of the wheels of the winch vehicle, simply and safely locks the vehicle in place, thereby preventing strain on the vehicle's transmission and braking system.

The 'Wedgits' may be used as a single pair in front of each wheel for hard and semi-soft ground, or doubled up for winching in very soft and boggy ground. By doubling up a pair of 'Wedgits' to each side of the vehicle one has in effect a long webbed foot which spreads the load.

These 'Wedgits' are made from heavy gauged steel and have a galvanised finish. They are available only from The Overlander Off Road Centre or one of their appointed stockists at £69.99 per pair plus carriage and VAT.

The second type of ground anchor developed by the company is for either anchoring a vehicle to its rear towing hook whilst winching, or alternatively, for attaching a winch rope whilst recovering onself with the vehicle's winch.

These ground anchors are known as T-Stakes because of their 'T' shaped section, designed for maximum strength, even in the softest of ground conditions. A heavy steel ring can be supplied for the attachment of the winch rope so that the pull is always at ground level. The top of the T-Stake is also equipped with a 'T-Bar' handle for removing the anchor from the ground after use.

Made of heavy steel, they are painted bright yellow so that they can be easily seen whilst in use. These two are only available from the Overlander Off Road Centre or appointed stockists at £39.99 per pair plus carriage and VAT. It is recommended that for extremely soft and sandy conditions two or three are used either in line or in a 'V' formation.

Overlander is at Zeal Monachorum, Nr. Crediton, Devon.

• *Wedgits can be doubled up for boggy ground (above) or used singly on harder ground (right).*

• *T-Stakes, designed for maximum strength, even in the softest of ground conditions.*

Fitting a Husky Electric Winch

ELECTRIC WINCHES fitted to Land Rovers are becoming increasingly popular, and with good reason. There are almost endless uses to winch a capable winch can be put, particularly if you work on the land.

Fitting an electric winch would, on the face of it, appear to be a complex task. But, with the complete kits now supplied by makers such as Superwinch Ltd the task is a relatively simple one.

A Husky winch kit contains everything you will need to fit it. All you will require is a modest tool kit.

Job number one is to remove the existing Land Rover front bumper and fit the specially constructed unit supplied. This is a straightforward bolt-on item.

With the new bumper in place, the electric leads are connected to the winch motor — the disconnected ends should be carefully labelled to avoid confusion once the winch is installed. The motor cover is then replaced and the fairlead rollers loosely mounted on the winch face.

At this point the winch is ready to be installed into the special bumper (paint the inside of the bumper with Hammerite before fitting the winch). With the Husky securely installed, the electric cables are fed into the engine bay and secured. A suitable spot must then be found to mount the relay.

This done, the cables are connected to the relay — the wisdom of labelling those cables, becomes apparent at this point! All that remains to be done is to connect the power supply to the relay direct from the battery — make sure it's up to the task, if not, buy a new one, and mount the socket for the hand control unit in a suitably accessible spot on the front of the vehicle.

With the winch installed and functioning the wire rope must be attached to the drum. This needs to be done carefully by winching in another vehicle ensuring that the cable is fed smoothly onto the drum.

That done, a short 'running in' period should be observed resulting in years of reliable performance from a very useful piece of equipment.

(Special thanks to the Overlander Centre, Devon).

Top: Everything you will need is included in the kit.
Left: Remove the original bumper and install the new one.
Below top: Connect the electric cables to the winch motor.
Bottom left: The winch is installed into the special bumper.
Below middle: The fairlead is mounted.
Bottom: The relay is fitted in a suitable spot inside the engine bay.

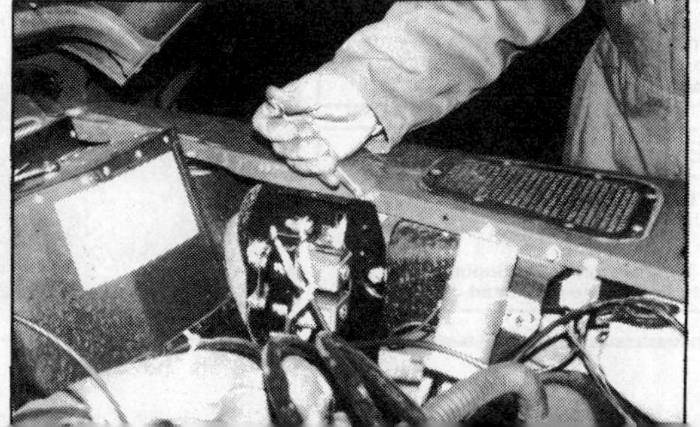

New mirr

ONE of the most irritating shortcomings of the early Range Rovers was the provision of second rate rear view door mirrors. The adjustment of the left side mirror is particularly inconvenient since the driver has to run round the outside of the car to get to it and it is the left mirror that is most usually knocked out of line by branches in the hedge.

I felt very envious of the Range Rover Vogues when they were introduced with their smart and functional electric mirrors that blend with the lines of the vehicle and are adjustable from within. Not only can they be adjusted left, right and up and down, but also have a heater circuit for defrosting or demisting.

I knew that the contour of the leading edge of the front door had remained the same from the old two door models, like my 1980 version, up to the present day four door models. Therefore, the triangular shaped base of the Vogue electric mirror should mount neatly on the older models provided that I could find a method of fixing it securely. This has not proved to be too difficult and can be undertaken by anyone who is reasonably competent with hand tools and has a little knowledge of car electrics.

The parts are easily obtained from a Land Rover dealer. Those for my mirror conversion came from the nearest Unipart shop. The finished job should look smart and be functional and it still allows free movement of the hinged front quarter light.

Preparing for the job

It took me the leisure time of one Sunday to do each separate mirror, so do allow enough time, or you can be driving around with your Range Rover in an illegal condition.

Unscrew the old door mirrors and pull out the rubber plugs from the door. Remove the lower carpeted side piece of trim from the inside of the door. The work might be accomplished more easily if the trim were removed from the upper part of the door also, but I was intimidated by the prospect of doing this and it is possible to manage without.

The triangular front corner piece of the two door Range Rover door frame is largely made of tough rubber reinforced internally by a small triangular black metal plate.

Below: the inside corner of the right door with filler paste and holes drilled.

ors for old

This plate is not strong enough to support the Vogue mirror assembly and needs to be prized out and discarded. Fill the triangular depression that removal of the plate reveals with epoxy resin paste filler up to the level of the surrounding black rubber.

The template printed below serves for marking the drilling sites in the door frame and for making the interior metal plate that goes inside each front door corner.

It is best to start by fashioning two of these plates out of metal sheet, which should be about 1.5 mm thick. I used aluminium alloy sheet for this purpose. I cut out this rather awkward shape with a fine round file blade in a hacksaw frame. Drill the holes and check that the three self tapping screws supplied with the Vogue mirror will pass through these holes and into the mirror base. The metal plate can then be held against the outside of the door frame to direct the drilling operation.

Note that the Vogue mirror base has to be aligned with the front edge of the frame of the two door model, whereas on the Range Rover Vogue the mirror base sits about 1 cm to the rear of the front edge.

Drilling the door frame

You are now ready to pass beyond the point of no return so a little care and thought is needed for each step. Hold the template in place and drill through each of the three holes into the door frame. The lower two holes are made easily and pass through the rubber and then through the hardened filler plate.

The upper hole is a little tricky since it goes partially through the steel door frame. It is best to begin with a smaller size of drill for this hole and then to enlarge the hole with a small round file, so that it can take the course directed by the template.

The mirror has a five wire flex and connecting plug from its base. This flex needs to be passed down inside the door. An adequate sized hole is needed to pass the plug through. This is cut into the rubber with a surgeon's or model maker's knife, where the hole will be completely concealed by the base of the mirror.

Begin by cutting into the lower part of the vertical rubber surface. Do not cut into the sill. This mining operation is carried out

Above: right hand control switch in the dash.

Above: a rocker switch and warning light for the heater circuit.

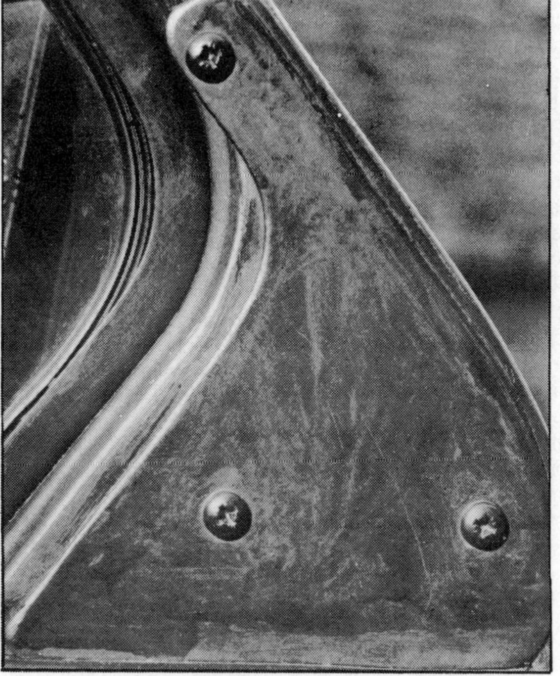

Above: metal plate fitted on the inside.

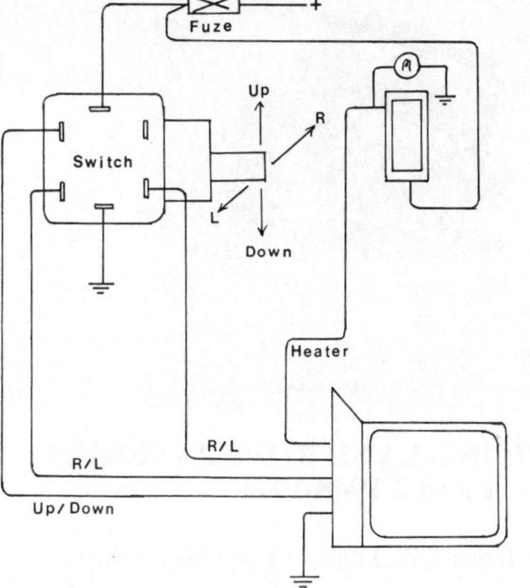

5mm

The template for making the inner metal plate and for hole drilling.

diagonally down until the door frame is encountered. Here you will need to change over to the electric drill to drill a passage that is then to be enlarged using a burr in the electric drill chuck.

Make the hole just large enough to pass the plug. You will have cut through both the aluminium and steel skins, so a bit of anti-corrosive paint around the edge of the hole is good practice.

Drop the plug through the hole and offer up the mirror base to the prepared site. You will see that there are three bosses protruding from the mirror base to take the self-tapping screws and you will need to perform a little more surgery on the rubber and filing or burr work on the outer edge of the steel window frame to let the bosses slip into place. The mirror base should eventually fit flush with the leading edge of the door frame in front and against the rubber trim of the door top edge below.

Place the metal plate on the inside of the door and pass the self-tapping screws through into the mirror base. The screws that are supplied are just long enough if washers are not used. Stand back and admire your work, but you still have to use resin filter paste to fill in the holes in the door and spray paint at a later date to mask the site of the old door holes.

Wiring

Each mirror has five wires. Four of these need connecting in the correct order to the control switches and the remaining wire goes to earth. In the Range Rover Vogue' control switches for mirror movement are located near the lighting switches in the steering column pod. It is probably not easy to install switches here; I did not attempt it and I have placed them in the dashboard right and left of the driving position, where they fall easily to hand. You will also need another switch for the heater circuit with a warning light or use a separate warning light.

Power is taken from a source that only becomes live when the ignition key is turned. I used the lead, located by the steering column, that the markers had provided to power the radio. Be sure to place a fuse holder and fuse somewhere in the power supply lead that you connect.

Power is taken to each of the two mirror movement switches and to the heater circuit switch. One terminal of each of the mirror movement switches has to be connected to earth. Leads from three of the remaining four terminals on these switches go the mirror.

For the heater switch, one side of the indicator light is connected to earth and the other side goes to the mirror.

Power from the switches to the mirrors can be taken by the wiring loom that a Land Rover dealer will supply for this purpose, but I decided that it would be more economic to do it myself and made my own connections. It takes a little while to sort out the connections to get the mirrors moving in the right direction and the mirror heater working, but it can all be done without sophisticated circuit testing equipment and is perfectly safe provided that you have remembered to install a fuse in the power circuit. Note that one connection from each mirror is to be connected to earth and this is for the heater circuit.

The wiring has to pass through to the door, for which Land Rover supply a rubber "elephant's trunk"and holes need to be made in the door and in the door pillar to take it. My Range Rover had already been fitted with door loud speakers, so I was able to pass the new wiring through the plastic spiral sheath that had been installed previously.

Inside the doors it is essential to use the short connecting lead that is supplied by Land Rover and is about a foot long. This is already fitted with a plug to mate with the one hanging down inside the door from the mirror. It is a rage inducing activity to pass the lead up inside the door and to join the connecting plugs with just one hand, but it can be done.

The Vogue mirrors were fitted to my Land Rover three years ago and have worked faultlessly since. The mounting method is evidently strong enough since a few trees have been hit, causing the mirrors to fold back on their spring hinges, but with no damage to the mounting. This has proved to be a very worthwhile improvement to a vehicle that is 'on the whole' not too easily battered.

Tools that are needed

Electric drill, burr for electric drill, surgeon's or model maker's knife, round files of various sizes, round file blade to fit hacksaw frame.

Parts that are needed

Template from Land Rover Owner, Range Rover Vogue electric mirrors (one left and one right), within door electric connector lead (standard Range Rover Vogue part), door speaker wiring sheath, 2 electric mirror switches, 1 rocker switch for heater circuit with warning light, 1 fuse and fuse holder, resin car repair paste, aluminium alloy sheet (or other metal) approx. 1.5 mm. thick, can of touch-up spray paint.